FAMILY AND MEDICAL LEAVE

IN A NUTSHELL

By

KURT H. DECKER

Adjunct Professor of Law
Widener University School of Law
Harrisburg, Pennsylvania
and
Adjunct Professor of Industrial Relations
Graduate School of Human Resource Management
and Industrial Relations
Saint Francis College
Loretto Pennsylvania
and
Partner
Stevens & Lee
Harrisburg, Lancaster, Lehigh Valley,
Philadelphia, Reading, Scranton, Valley Forge, and
Wilkes Barre, Pennsylvania
and Wilmington, Delaware
and
Cherry Hill, New Jersey

WEST GROUP

ST. PAUL, MINN.
2000

TEXT IS PRINTED ON 10% POST
CONSUMER RECYCLED PAPER

For Hilary and all other working spouses

who value the role

of family in a civilized society

*

PREFACE

Increasingly, America's children and elderly are dependent upon family members who must spend long hours at work. When a family emergency arises, requiring employees to attend to seriously-ill children or parents, or to newly-born or adopted infants, or even to their own serious illness, employees need reassurance that they will not be asked to choose between continuing their employment, meeting their personal and family obligations, or tending to vital needs at home.

The Family Medical and Leave Act (FMLA) was enacted on February 5, 1993, to allow employees the opportunity to balance their work and family life by taking reasonable unpaid leaves. It is intended to balance the workplace's demands with the needs of families, to promote the stability and economic security of families, and to promote national interests in preserving family integrity.

The FMLA allows eligible employees of a covered employer to take job-protected, unpaid leave, or to substitute appropriate paid leave if the employee has earned or accrued it, for up to a total of twelve workweeks in any twelve months for:

1. The birth of a child and to care for the newborn child;

2. The placement of a child with the employee for adoption or foster care;

3. The care of a family member (child, spouse, or parent) with a serious health condition; or

4. The employee's own serious health condition which makes the employee unable to perform his or her job functions.

In certain cases, this leave may be taken on an intermittent basis rather than all at once. The employee may also work a part-time or reduced leave schedule.

An employee on FMLA leave is also entitled to have health benefits maintained while on leave. If an employee was paying all or part of the premium payments prior to the leave, the employee would continue to pay his or her share during the leave. The employer may recover its share only if the employee does not return to work for a reason other than the serious health condition of the employee or of the employee's immediate family member, or another reason beyond the employee's control.

An employee generally has a right to return to the same or an equivalent position with equivalent pay, benefits, and working conditions at the leave's conclusion. Taking FMLA leave cannot result in the loss of any benefit that accrued prior to the leave's start.

The FMLA is a significant piece of legislation that daily affects the workplace. Because of its complexity, however, it is not easily understood.

This Nutshell can be used as a free standing or as a supplementary text for courses in discrimination, employment and labor law, labor standards legislation, and recent developments in employment law by law schools and graduate schools offering business administration, human resource management, and industrial relations curriculums. It can also be used by practitioners, including human resource managers and attorneys, as a daily reference guide for dealing with FMLA issues.

Chapter 1 introduces the family and medical leave concept as the backgound for federal and state legislative action. The federal Family and Medical Leave Act (FMLA) of 1993 is reviewed in Chapter 2. An overview of state family and medical leave regulation is provided in Chapter 3. Benefits, leave types, and return to employment are examined in Chapter 4. Significant court decisions that have interpreted the FMLA are presented in Chapter 5. Finally, Chapter 6 illustrates the procedures, policies, and forms that an employer should consider in implementing and administering the FMLA.

Little in life is a solitary undertaking. Much is a culmination of other people's thoughts and efforts. This Nutshell is no different. In preparing this Nutshell, many individuals either provided opportunities or shared their knowledge. Among these were

Dr. Robert D. Lee, Jr. of the Pennsylvania State University in giving hope that a future existed after military service by pursuing a graduate education, Dr. William E. Caldwell of the Pennsylvania State University for nurturing an interest in employment law, Professor Paul H. Sanders of Vanderbilt University School of Law for instilling the recognition for conflict resolution's importance in employment law, Professor Robert N. Covington of Vanderbilt University School of Law for his friendship and wise counsel over the years, Dr. Harry Kershen for affording the first opportunity to appear in print, Dr. Edwin Wagner and Dr. Philip Benham of the Graduate School of Human Resource Management and Industrial Relations of Saint Francis College for encouraging the sharing of knowledge through teaching, Dean John Gedid and Dean Loren K. Prescott of Widener University School of Law (Harrisburg) for recognizing the evolving area of individual employment rights' importance to the law school curriculum, H. Thomas Felix, II, Esq. of Montgomery, McCracken, Walker & Rhoads and Arbitrator John M. Skonier, for their continued encouragement of my employment law research, writing, and teaching interests, and Sidney D. Kline, Esq. and Joseph M. Harenza, Esq. of Stevens & Lee for their support over the years in pursuing academic interests outside of the law firm's normal client responsibilities.

As this Nutshell is completed, I am struck with an awareness that even though this is an introductory undertaking to family and medical leave that it will never truly be finished as society reevaluates the role of family and work. There is much yet to be researched, learned, and analyzed as we become ever more conscious of this highly important area that affects us all as we journey through life.

The words were said best by historian Barbara W. Tuchman in her introduction to *The Proud Tower*:

> I realize what follows offers no overall conclusion . . . I also know that what follows is far from the whole picture. It is not false modesty which prompts me to say so but simply an acute awareness of what I have not included. The faces and voices of all that I have left out crowd around me as I reach the end.

This is, then, not the final word on family and medical leave. As legislatures and courts evaluate and potentially expand this concept, I hope that I will be given the opportunity to refine the principles set forth in this Nutshell.

KURT H. DECKER

Reading, Pennsylvania
August 1999

*

OUTLINE

OUTLINE

Page

OUTLINE

*

TABLE OF CASES

References are to Pages

TABLE OF CASES

*

FAMILY AND MEDICAL LEAVE
IN A NUTSHELL

*

CHAPTER 1

THE FAMILY AND MEDICAL LEAVE CONCEPT: AN INTRODUCTION TO FEDERAL AND STATE LEGISLATIVE ACTION

A. INTRODUCTION

Prior to the Family and Medical Leave Act's (FMLA's) enactment in 1993, employers were not required by a federal statute to provide leave for family or medical purposes. Pub. L. No. 103–3, 107 Stat. 6 (1993); *codified at* 2 U.S.C.A. §§ 1301, 1302, 1312, 1381–1385, 1401–1416; 5 U.S.C.A. §§ 6381–6387; 29 U.S.C.A. §§ 2601, 2611–2619, 2631–2636, 2651–2654. The family and medical leave concept was not new. Over thirty states had already adopted legislation mandating some form of family and/or medical leave. This state legislation provided leaves for adoption, child rearing, maternity, sickness of the employee, sickness of the employee's family, etc. Many employers also voluntarily provided some form of this leave to employees.

As females, single mothers, and dual income families expanded the United States' predominantly

1

male workforce during the 1960s through 1990s, legislative attention began to be focused on balancing employment with family and medical needs. If employees were treated fairly in these matters, they would be more productive. U.S. businesses could also compete more effectively in the rapidly emerging global economy where these issues had already been addressed.

The FMLA was adopted to assure employee job security for taking care of family and medical responsibilities on a national level. This chapter provides an overview of the reasons and the historical framework for family and medical leave legislation at the national and state levels along with identifying possible future changes. It reviews the:

1. Changing workplace;

2. New demands on families and employees for family and medical leave;

3. Legislative responses throughout the world and in the United States; and

4. Future family and medical leave considerations.

B. THE CHANGING WORKPLACE

Much of the rationale and legislative history for the FMLA's adoption is set forth in its legislative history. REPORT FROM THE COMMITTEE ON LABOR AND HUMAN RESOURCES, S. Rep. No. 3, 103d Cong., 1st Sess. 1–51 (1993) [hereinafter FMLA LEGISLATIVE HISTORY REPORT]. The

FMLA's legislative history is valuable in understanding the reasons for the FMLA and what future directions this concept may take.

The United States is fast becoming a society where both sexes work. Over two-thirds of adult females are employed, and over half of the mothers with children are employed full-time. Two-thirds of the new workforce entrants before 2000 will be females and two-thirds of all preschool children will have mothers working outside the home. FMLA LEGISLATIVE HISTORY REPORT at 49.

Private sector practices and government policies have failed to respond to these economic and social changes that have intensified the tensions between employment and family. This failure imposes a heavy burden on employers, employees, families, and the broader society. Some form of family and medical leave was necessary to respond to the growing conflict between employment and family. FMLA LEGISLATIVE HISTORY REPORT at 4.

Employees should not be required to choose between careers and families. They need to remain employed for earning sufficient income to:

1. Raise their families;

2. Have children;

3. Tend to their children's needs; and

4. Care for sick children and ailing parents.

Balancing is required to accommodate the family's needs and the workplace's demands.

Family and medical leave supports these needs and demands. Employers offering these benefits may:

1. Remain competitive in the employment marketplace;

2. Recruit and retain better employees; and

3. Improve employee productivity, particularly when skilled-labor shortages exist.

Family and medical leave lessens the concerns of employees with young children and aging parents. Its benefits help ease the transition from welfare to employment for low-income and disadvantaged families. FMLA LEGISLATIVE HISTORY REPORT at 49.

C. THE NEW DEMANDS ON FAMILIES AND EMPLOYEES

1. CHANGE IN THE WORKFORCE'S COMPOSITION

Since the mid–1950s, the United States has experienced a demographic revolution in its workforce's composition. Today, according to the Bureau of Labor Statistics (BLS), ninety-six percent of fathers and sixty-five percent of mothers work outside the home. This change in the workplace's composition has had and will continue to have consequences on employees and their families. FMLA LEGISLATIVE HISTORY REPORT at 6.

The need for job protected family and medical leave arose before these changes in the workforce's composition occurred. Employees and their families have always been affected when a family member lost employment for family or medical reasons.

These employment losses are felt more today because of the rise in single heads of households who are predominantly female employees in low paid jobs. For these females and their children, employment loss from family commitments or illness can have devastating economic consequences by eliminating the income source that supports the family. FMLA LEGISLATIVE HISTORY REPORT at 7.

These demographic changes have been far reaching. With males and females as wage earners, the crucial unpaid caretaking services traditionally performed by spouses in the past; i.e, care of young children, ill family members, and aging parents, has become increasingly difficult for families to provide or fulfill. When there is no one to offer this care, individuals can be permanently affected as these basic human needs remain unfilled.

Families unable to perform their essential functions can be undermined and weakened. When families fail, the community is left to cope with the consequences of dealing with emotionally and physically weakened children and adults.

2. FEMALES IN THE WORKPLACE

Female participation in the workforce was nineteen percent in 1900. Today, more than forty-five percent of the United States' workforce are females.

Of this forty-five percent, females are distributed as follows:

1. Seventy-four percent are females aged 25–54;

2. Fifty-six percent are mothers with children under the age of six; and

3. Fifty-one percent are mothers with children under the age of one. FMLA LEGISLATIVE HISTORY REPORT at 6.

The General Accounting Office reported that since the 1950s, the female private sector labor force increased by about a million employees each year. Since 1979, females accounted for more than three-fifths or sixty-two percent of the increase in the private sector labor force.

By 1990, nearly fifty-seven million females were employed or searching for employment. This constitutes a more than 200 percent increase in the female workforce since 1950. FMLA LEGISLATIVE HISTORY REPORT at 5.

By 2000, it is expected that two out of three new workforce entrants will be females. The Bureau of Labor Statistics (BLS) predicts that by 2005, that the female workforce participation rate will reach almost sixty-six percent. FMLA LEGISLATIVE HISTORY REPORT at 5, 6.

3.   SINGLE–PARENT HOUSEHOLDS

Divorce, separation, and out-of-wedlock births have required millions of females as single heads of households to support themselves and their children. These females often cannot keep their families above the poverty level. A mother's employment is often required to keep the family intact. FMLA LEGISLATIVE HISTORY REPORT at 7.

4. PARENTAL CARE RESPONSIBILITIES

Due to the advances in medical technology and health care, Americans are living longer. The fastest growing segment of the American population is the elderly. Many of these elderly also have younger children who are employees. FMLA LEGISLATIVE HISTORY REPORT at 6.

Removing people from a home environment has been shown to be costly and often detrimental to the health and well-being of persons with mental and physical disabilities. This has caused a trend away from institutionalization.

Independent parental living situations can result in increased care responsibilities for family members. Many of these caregiving family members are by necessity also employees. Home care to fulfill parental responsibilities can add to the tension between employment demands and family needs.

The percentage of adults in the care of their employed children or parents due to physical and mental disabilities is becoming more significant. The need to deal with the serious illness of the parent often creates a crisis for the employee and the entire family. During this time, the following are often at a premium for the employee with caregiving responsibilities:

1. A stable income;

2. The assurance of a secure position; and

3. The opportunity to take time off when necessary. FMLA LEGISLATIVE HISTORY REPORT at 10.

5.   CHILD–CARE RESPONSIBILITIES

Many new parents have no guarantee that their employment will be protected because of child-care responsibilities. This may occur when they are unable to work:

1. Due to pregnancy, child-birth, or related medical conditions;

2. After childbirth; or

3. After placement for adoption or foster care when they need to stay home to care for their infants.

Adoptive parents also face difficulties. Most adoption agencies require the presence of a parent in the home immediately after the adoption. Some require this presence for as long as four months. This time period is needed to ensure adequate time for proper bonding between the adoptive parent and child. FMLA LEGISLATIVE HISTORY REPORT at 7–8.

6.   THE EMPLOYEE'S SERIOUS HEALTH CONDITION

Employees should not be subject to arbitrary terminations when they are confronted with a serious illness and are not capable of working. Employment loss because of illness has a particularly devastating effect on employees who support themselves and on families where two incomes are necessary or where a single parent heads the household. FMLA LEGISLATIVE HISTORY REPORT at 11.

D.   FAMILY AND MEDICAL LEAVE LEGISLATION

1.   WORLDWIDE LEGISLATION

Prior to adopting the Family and Medical Leave Act (FMLA) in 1993, the United States was one of the few remaining industrialized nations that had not enacted legislation setting family and medical leave standards. Pub. L. No. 103–3, 107 Stat. 6 (1993); *codified at* 2 U.S.C.A. § 1312, 5 U.S.C.A. §§ 6381–6387, 29 U.S.C.A. §§ 2601, 2611–2619, 2631–2636, 2651–2654. All of the United States' major global competitors provide some form of leave for these purposes. Much of this leave is paid. In addition, many Third World countries have national policies that provide some form of maternity or parental leave. FMLA LEGISLATIVE HISTORY REPORT at 19–20.

Among the major industrialized nations, the average minimum paid leave is twelve to fourteen weeks with many also providing the right to unpaid, job-protected leaves for at least one year. Leave is provided either through a national paid sick leave system or as part of a national policy designed to enhance and support families.

One hundred and thirty five nations provide minimum maternity benefits. One hundred and twenty seven nations offer some form of wage replacement. These policies are well established.

France, Great Britain, and Italy had legislation requiring maternity benefits prior to World War I. These benefits are now part of the general paid sick leave laws providing benefits for all employees unable to work for medical reasons. In 1992, the European Community Commission issued a directive requiring that all of its member nations provide a standard minimum of fourteen weeks paid maternity leave.

Japan provides twelve weeks of partially paid pregnancy disability leave. In Canada, females may take maternity leave for up to forty-one weeks and receive sixty percent of their salary for the first fifteen weeks.

Sweden guarantees leave for eighteen months of family leave at approximately ninety percent of the employee's gross pay. Either parent can use the leave, but not at the same time. Swedes are encouraged to use part of the leave when a child is born and to save the rest to help the child make the transition into school at age seven. A parent of a child under the age of eight is entitled to as many as ninety sick days a year to care for the child's illness. Contrary to the widely held belief that employees would abuse a liberal leave policy, the average usage rate of this leave is seven days a year.

Several nations also provide leave for elder care. In Norway, employees can take paid leave equal to their income covered by pensions for up to one month a year to care for close relatives who are terminally ill. In Austria, paid leave of up to one week a year is available to care for a sick relative.

Great Britain, France, and Luxembourg all have leave standards providing time off for care of an aged parent. Many of the industrialized nations that do not have specific leave policies to cover elder care have elaborate and generous long-term health care systems. FMLA LEGISLATIVE HISTORY RE-PORT at 19–20.

2.   STATE FAMILY AND MEDICAL LEAVE LEGISLATION

Over thirty states, the District of Columbia, and Puerto Rico have adopted some form of family and/or medical leave. FMLA LEGISLATIVE HIS-TORY REPORT at 20–21; see also Chapter 3. Over half of the states have legislation requiring employers to provide family and/or medical leave in certain circumstances. Most of these statutes apply only to state employees. These are often part of general personnel or civil service statutes governing the state.

3.   THE FEDERAL FAMILY AND MEDICAL LEAVE ACT OF 1993

The Family and Medical Leave Act (FMLA) of 1993 is the federal government's response to the growing tension between family and work. Pub. L. No. 103–3, 107 Stat. 6 (1993); *codified at* 2 U.S.C.A. § 1312, 5 U.S.C.A. §§ 6381–6387, 29 U.S.C.A. §§ 2601, 2611–2619, 2631–2636, 2651–2654; see also Chapters 2, 4–6. It establishes a right to unpaid family and medical leave for employees covered by its provisions.

Increasingly, children and elderly are dependent for care upon family members who must spend long hours at work. When a family emergency arises, requiring employees to attend to seriously-ill children or parents, or to newly-born or adopted infants, or even to their own serious illness, employees need reassurance that they must not choose between:

1.   Continuing their employment;

2.   Meeting their personal and family obligations; or

3.   Tending to vital needs at home.

The FMLA's enactment was predicated on these needs of today's workforce.

Family and medical leave legislation was debated at the national level since the mid–1980s. Congress passed several family and medical leave bills in the late 1980s; however, all were vetoed by President George H. Bush.

The FMLA of 1993 was introduced in the House of Representatives in January 1993, and was passed by the Senate on February 4, 1993. It was signed into law by President William J. Clinton on February 5, 1993.

The FMLA's provisions cover more than fifty million employees in the private sector, and three hundred thousand United States businesses. Those employed in state and local governments total another fifteen million employees.

The FMLA's purposes are to:

1. Balance the demands of the workplace with the needs of families;

2. Promote the stability and economic security of families; and

3. Promote national interests in preserving family integrity. 29 U.S.C.A. § 2601(b).

The FMLA attempts to balance the employer's legitimate interests for an efficient workplace with the employee's family and medical needs. It also seeks to minimize the potential for employment discrimination based on sex in promoting equal employment opportunity for males and females.

The FMLA's legislative history indicates that a direct correlation exists between family stability and workplace productivity. FMLA LEGISLATIVE HISTORY REPORT at 1–51. A stable employment relationship and the comparatively small costs of guaranteeing that this relationship will not be disturbed while employees attend to important family and medical obligations support the FMLA's adoption. This benefits employees and employers.

The FMLA entitles an "eligible employee" to take up to a total of twelve workweeks of unpaid leave during any twelve-month period for:

1. The birth of a child and to care for this child;

2. For the placement of a child for adoption or foster care;

3. The care for a spouse or an immediate family member with a serious health condition; or

4. A serious health condition that makes the employee unable to perform the functions of his or her position. 29 U.S.C.A. § 2612(a)(1).

Employers are required to maintain any pre-existing group health coverage during the leave period. 29 U.S.C.A. § 2614(c)(1). Once the leave period is concluded the employer is required to reinstate the employee to the same or an equivalent position with equivalent employment benefits, pay, and other terms and conditions of employment. 29 U.S.C.A. § 2614(a).

The Department of Labor (DOL) administers the FMLA. It provides a hotline to employees and employers who may have questions about the FMLA by telephoning 1–800–959–FMLA or the DOL's Web site pages can be accessed at:

1. http://www.dol.gov/dol/esa/fmla.htm or

2. http://www.dol.gov/elaws.

E. FUTURE FAMILY AND MEDICAL LEAVE CONSIDERATIONS

1. THE COMMISSION ON FAMILY AND MEDICAL LEAVE'S REPORT

The Commission on Family and Medical Leave was a bi-partisan group established pursuant to the FMLA's Title III. 29 U.S.C.A. §§ 2631–2636. It contracted with two independent research firms to conduct two surveys. REPORT OF THE COMMISSION ON FAMILY AND MEDICAL LEAVE, A WORKABLE BALANCE: REPORT TO THE CONGRESS ON FAMILY AND MEDICAL LEAVE POLICIES (April 30, 1996) [hereinafter FMLA COMMISSION'S REPORT]. The surveys conducted addressed the:

1. Use of FMLA leave and

2. The FMLA's effect on employees.

In April 1996, the Commission released its results. A summary follows:

a. Pre–FMLA Leave Policies

Sixty-nine percent of employers indicated that they had some form of family and medical leave policies in place before the FMLA's adoption in 1993. FMLA COMMISSION'S REPORT at ch. 3. The employers' reasons for providing this leave included:

1. A desire to help employees balance family and work demands;

2. Employee requests;

3. A state mandate;

4. Changing workforce demographics;

5. Cost-effectiveness;

6. Retention of valued employees; and

7. Competitiveness with other employers. FMLA COMMISSION'S REPORT at ch. 3.

Sixty-five percent of the employers indicated that their pre-FMLA leave policy was uniform throughout the organization. Sixty-eight percent permitted intermittent leave as part of their policy. FMLA COMMISSION'S REPORT at ch. 3.

The typical amount of leave was twelve weeks. More employers were likely to have provided unpaid leave than paid leave. FMLA COMMISSION'S REPORT at ch. 3.

Leave was available almost equally to male and female employees with the exception of childbirth. Eighty-six percent of the employers indicated that leave was available for females for the birth of a child. Only fifty-nine percent reported that leave was available for males for the birth of a child. In addition, thirty-five percent indicated that leave was available for the illness of a "significant other." FMLA COMMISSION'S REPORT at ch. 3.

b. Awareness of the FMLA

Eighty-six percent of the employers knew they were covered by the FMLA. FMLA COMMISSION'S REPORT at ch. 4.

c. Use of FMLA Leave

One major conclusion was that approximately forty-seven percent of the employees in the private sector were eligible to take leave under the FMLA, but only two to four percent actually took an FMLA leave since January 1994. This may be because the FMLA is unpaid. FMLA COMMISSION'S REPORT at ch. 7.

The following FMLA usage patterns emerged:

1. *Female versus Male Leave Takers*: Fifty-eight percent of FMLA leaves were taken by females.

2. *Largest Group of Leave Takers' Age*: Forty-one percent or the largest group of FMLA leave takers was between ages 35 to 49.

3. *Common Reason for Leaves*:

   a. Fifty-nine percent took an FMLA leave for their own serious health condition and

   b. Nineteen percent took an FMLA leave to care for a seriously ill child, spouse, or parent.

4. *Leave Length*: Fifty percent of the FMLA leave takers took fewer than ten days. FMLA COMMISSION'S REPORT at ch. 7.

d. The Impact on Employee Morale

Eighty-two percent of the employers indicated that the FMLA had no effect on employee morale. Only eighteen percent said that it had actually improved morale. FMLA COMMISSION'S REPORT at ch. 7.

e. Employer Leave Policies

Two-thirds of FMLA-covered employers revised their then current leave policies to comply with the FMLA. FMLA COMMISSION'S REPORT at ch. 4. Employers revised their leave policies regarding:

1. *Reasons for Leave*: Seventy-seven percent increased the number of reasons leave could be taken.

2. *Male Eligibility*: Seventy percent allowed males to take leave for sick, newborn, or newly adopted children.

3. *Leave Length*: Sixty-seven percent increased the length of permitted leaves.

4. *Continuation of Benefits*: Fifty-three percent continued health insurance during the leave. FMLA COMMISSION'S REPORT at ch. 4.

Some states have leave policies that have more expansive standards than the federal FMLA. Seventy-eight percent of the employers that did business in more than one state adopted the more expansive standards for the state with these policies only. Twenty-two percent adopted the more expansive standards for all their employees regardless of state. FMLA COMMISSION'S REPORT at ch. 3.

f. Employer Communication

Employers communicated FMLA leave information to employees by:

1. *Notice Posting*: Ninety-four percent posted notices.

2. *Employee Handbook*: Forty-seven percent placed information in the employee handbook.

3. *Supervisor Communication*: Thirty-nine percent made the employees' supervisor responsible for disseminating the policy.

4. *Informational Meetings*: Eighteen percent communicated via informational meetings. FMLA COMMISSION'S REPORT at ch. 3.

Employers also reported that they communicated FMLA leave policies by newsletter to employees and distributed their policy to employees.

g. The Return-to-Work Rate

Where at least one employee had taken an FMLA leave since January 1, 1994, thirty-three percent had employees who did not return to work from the leave. FMLA COMMISSION'S REPORT at ch. 5. Only seven percent attempted to recover health insurance premiums paid for these employees during the leave. FMLA COMMISSION'S REPORT at ch. 5.

h. Administration Costs

The FMLA's opponents were concerned about the cost of administering it. Early survey results, however, suggest that these costs have not been as great as anticipated. FMLA COMMISSION'S REPORT at ch. 6.

Between eighty-nine and ninety-eight percent of employers reported that no or only small costs were associated with the FMLA's:

1. Administration;

2. Hiring and training; or

3. Continuing benefits. FMLA COMMISSION'S REPORT at ch. 6.

Eighty-one percent reported that the cost of the program was so minimal that they had no formal process in place to account for it. The employers' estimates were as follows:

1. *Unknown or Not Measured*: Forty-seven percent.

2. *Zero Additional Cost Incurred*: Twenty-three percent.

3. *Incidental, Negligible, or Minimal Costs Incurred*: Eleven percent. FMLA COMMISSION'S REPORT at ch. 6.

Overall, about ninety percent of employers reported no or minimal compliance costs. However, a significant minority of respondents, especially large employers, reported nagging administrative costs. FMLA COMMISSION'S REPORT at ch. 6.

Responding employers estimated that the administration costs incurred were associated with the following:

1. *Personnel Costs*: Twenty-two percent indicated that they had incurred personnel costs, including hiring new personnel to

handle FMLA paperwork or the promotion of an employee to handle the paperwork. When asked specifically how many new employees had been hired to handle FMLA administrative responsibilities, only one employer indicated that it had hired an additional professional employee and one other employer reported that it had hired an additional part-time clerical employee.

2. *Lost Work Time*: Nineteen percent provided information concerning lost work since the FMLA went into effect in 1993. The range of lost time was from one to seven total months, with a mean of a little over four months per employer and a median of five months per employer.

3. *Other Costs*: Other costs employers incurred were:

   a. Consulting advice;

   b. Overtime to cover for employees on leave;

   c. Benefits for employees on leave;

   d. Expense of notifying employees of the policy; and

   e. Tracking for DOL audit requests.

4. *Program Administration*: Employers reported costs associated with the:

   a. Time spent by their current staff in program administration and

b.   Time spent by the human resources manager that had to be diverted from other activities to FMLA issues. FMLA COMMISSION'S REPORT at ch. 6.

Managing intermittent leaves was the most common employer complaint.

2. PROPOSED LEGISLATION

As of 1999, federal legislation pointed toward expanding the FMLA coverage and benefits through the following pending bills in the House of Representatives and the Senate:

1. *The Family and Medical Leave Improvements Act* (H.R. 91, 106th Cong.). This bill expands the FMLA's coverage to employers with 25 employees within a 75 mile radius. It would also amend the FMLA to allow employees to take 24 hours of FMLA leave within a twelve month period to participate in a child's school activities and to accompany their children and elderly relatives to routine medical and dental appointments.

2. *Family and Medical Leave Fairness Act* (S. 201, 106th Cong.). This bill expands the FMLA's coverage to employers with 25 employees within a 75 mile radius.

CHAPTER 2

THE FEDERAL FAMILY AND MEDICAL LEAVE ACT (FMLA): AN OVERVIEW

A. INTRODUCTION

On February 5, 1993, the Family and Medical Leave Act (FMLA) was signed into law by President William J. Clinton. Pub. L. No. 103–3, 107 Stat. 6 (1993); *codified at* 2 U.S.C.A. §§ 1301, 1302, 1312, 1381–1385, 1401–1416; 5 U.S.C.A. §§ 6381–6387; 29 U.S.C.A. §§ 2601–2654. The FMLA conferred a number of new rights on eligible employees. It also created new obligations for covered employers.

Under the FMLA, employees who qualify may be entitled to as much as twelve weeks of unpaid leave under certain circumstances. This chapter discusses the FMLA's major statutory provisions that affect employees and employers.

B. COVERAGE

The FMLA has six titles. Five of these titles refer specifically to family and medical leave. The last title directs the Secretary of the Department of Defense to review its policies regarding the service of homosexuals in the armed forces. These six titles are:

Title I, General Requirements for Leave. Covers most private employers. It describes the reasons allowed for leave, duration of leaves and reinstatements, and obligations of employers and employees, and it provides definitions of the FMLA's key terms. 29 U.S.C.A. §§ 2601–2619.

Title II, Leave for Federal Civil Service Employees. Provides the same type of information as Title I but covers federal civil service employees. 5 U.S.C.A. §§ 6381–6387.

Title III, Commission on Leave. Established a bipartisan commission to investigate and prepare a report regarding the FMLA's impact on employers and employees, to review the state laws, and to investigate potential additional legislation to provide leave benefits for employees not covered by the FMLA. The Commission, chaired by Senator Christopher Dodd (D–Conn.), disbanded in 1996 following completion of its investigation and report. 29 U.S.C.A. §§ 2631–2636.

Title IV, Miscellaneous Provisions. Includes provisions for integrating the FMLA with state laws, a statement of non-discrimination, and establishment of regulations by the Department of Labor (DOL). 29 U.S.C.A. §§ 2651–2654.

Title V, Coverage of Congressional Employees. Provides for similar coverage for Senate and House employees and describes a few areas of distinction from Titles I and II. 2 U.S.C.A. §§ 1301, 1302, 1312, 1381–1385.

Title VI, Sense of Congress. A rider that requires the Secretary of the Department of Defense to review its policies with respect to the service of homosexuals in the armed forces. Pub. L. No. 103–3, 107 Stat. 6, § 601 (Feb. 5, 1993).

In adopting the FMLA, Congress specifically found that:

1. The number of single-parent households and two-parent households in which the single parent or both parents work was increasing significantly;

2. It was important for the development of children and the family that mothers and fathers be able to participate in early childrearing and the care of family members who had serious health conditions;

3. The lack of employment policies to accommodate working parents could force individuals to choose between job security and parenting;

4. There was inadequate job security for employees who had serious health conditions that prevented them from working for temporary periods;

5. Due to the nature of the roles of females and males in society, the primary responsibility for family caretaking often fell on females, and this responsibility affected the working

lives of females more than it affected males; and

6. Employment standards that applied to one gender only had serious potential for encouraging employers to discriminate against employees and applicants for employment who were of that gender. 29 U.S.C.A. § 2601(a).

In turn, the FMLA's purposes are to:

1. Balance workplace demands with family needs;

2. Promote the family's stability and economic security;

3. Promote national interests by preserving family integrity;

4. Entitle employees to take a reasonable leave for:

    a. Medical reasons;

    b. The birth or adoption of a child; and

    c. The care of a child, spouse, or parent who has a serious health condition;

5. Accomplish the FMLA's purposes in a manner that accommodates employers' legitimate interests;

6. Accomplish the FMLA's purposes in a manner that, consistent with the Equal Protection Clause of the United States Constitution's Fourteenth Amendment, minimizes the potential for employment discrimination on the basis of sex by ensuring generally that leave

is available for eligible medical reasons, including maternity-related disability, and for compelling family reasons, on a gender neutral basis; and

7. Promote the goal of equal opportunity for females and males. 29 U.S.C.A. § 2601(b).

C. TITLE I–GENERAL REQUIREMENTS FOR FMLA LEAVE

1. TITLE I—GENERALLY

The FMLA's Title I covers most private employers. It describes:

1. The reasons allowed for leave;

2. Duration of leaves and reinstatements;

3. Obligations of employers and employees; and

4. Definitions of the FMLA's key terms. 29 U.S.C.A. §§ 2601–2619.

2. DEFINITIONS

The FMLA's definitions are critical to its understanding, interpretation, and application. Among other things, these definitions determine employee eligibility for FMLA leave and employer coverage. They are as follows:

a. Commerce, Industry, or Activity Affecting Commerce. 29 U.S.C.A. § 2611(1).

This definition extends federal jurisdiction for the FMLA's application and enforcement to:

1. Interstate commerce between the states;

2. The District of Columbia; and

3. Territories of the United States.

"Commerce" means:

1. Any activity, business, or industry in commerce or

2. A labor dispute that would hinder or obstruct commerce or the free flow of commerce.

"Any industry affecting commerce" and "commerce" are to be interpreted as defined in the Labor Management Relations Act (LMRA) of 1947. See 29 U.S.C.A. §§ 142(1), 142(3).

The LMRA defines "any industry affecting commerce" as any industry or activity in commerce or in which a labor dispute would burden or obstruct commerce or tend to burden or obstruct commerce or the free flow of commerce. 29 U.S.C.A. § 142(1).

"Commerce" is defined under the LMRA as this term is used under the National Labor Relations Act (NLRA). See 29 U.S.C.A. § 142(3). The NLRA defines "commerce" as trade, traffic, commerce, transportation, or communication:

1. Among the states;

2. Between the District of Columbia or any territory of the United States and any state or other territory;

3. Between any foreign country and any state, territory, or the District of Columbia; or

4. Within the District of Columbia or any territory; or

5. Between points in the same state but through any other state or any territory or the District of Columbia or any foreign country. 29 U.S.C.A. § 152(6).

b. Eligible Employee. 29 U.S.C.A. § 2611(2).

An eligible employee means an employee who has been employed:

1. For at least twelve months by the employer and

2. For at least 1,250 hours of service with this employer during the previous twelve month period.

However, eligible employee does not include:

1. Any federal officer or employee covered under subchapter V of chapter 63 of title 5, United States Code [see 5 U.S.C.A. § 6381] or

2. Any employee of an employer who is employed at a worksite at which this employer employs less than 50 employees if the total number of employees employed by that employer within 75 miles of that worksite is less than 50.

c. Employ, Employee, State. 29 U.S.C.A. § 2611(3).

These terms are given the same meaning as used under the Fair Labor Standards Act (FLSA). See 29 U.S.C.A. §§ 203(c), 203(e), 203(g). The FLSA defines "employ" as including to suffer or permit to work. 29 U.S.C.A. § 203(g).

"Employee" is defined under the FLSA as any individual employed by an employer. 29 U.S.C.A. § 203(e). It does not include any individual who volunteers to perform services for a public agency which is a state, a political subdivision of a state, or an interstate governmental agency, if:

1.   The individual receives no compensation or is paid expenses, reasonable benefits, or a nominal fee to perform the services for which the individual volunteers and

2.   These services are not the same type of services which the individual is employed to perform for the public agency.

However, an employee of a public agency which is a state, political subdivision of a state, or an interstate governmental agency may volunteer to perform services for any other state, political subdivision, or interstate governmental agency, including a state, political subdivision, or agency with which the employing state, political subdivision, or agency has a mutual aid agreement.

"State" under the FLSA means any state of the United States or the District of Columbia or any territory or possession of the United States. 29 U.S.C.A. § 203(c).

d. Employer. 29 U.S.C.A. § 2611(4).

An employer is any person who is engaged in commerce or in any industry affecting commerce who employs fifty or more employees for each working day during each of twenty or more calendar workweeks in the current or preceding calendar year. It includes any:

1. Person who acts, directly, or indirectly, in the employer's interest to any of the employees of that employer;

2. Successor in interest of an employer; and

3. Public agency as defined under the Fair Labor Standards Act (FLSA). See 29 U.S.C.A. § 203(x). A public agency is considered engaged in commerce or in an industry or activity affecting commerce for the FMLA's purposes. Under the FLSA, "public agency" means:

   a. The government of the United States;

   b. The government of a state or political subdivision of this state;

   c. Any agency of the United States, including the United States Postal Service and Postal Rate Commission;

   d. A state;

   e. A political subdivision of a state; or

   f. Any interstate governmental agency. 29 U.S.C.A. § 203(x).

e. Employment Benefits. 29 U.S.C.A. § 2611(5).

Employment benefits are all the benefits that are provided or made available to employees by an employer. It makes no difference whether these benefits are provided by a practice or written employer policy or through an "employee benefit plan" as defined in the Employee Retirement Income Security Act of 1974 (ERISA). See 29 U.S.C.A. § 1002(3).

Under ERISA, this means an employee welfare benefit plan, an employee pension benefit plan, or a plan that is both an employee welfare benefit plan and an employee pension benefit plan. These benefits include, but are not limited to:

1. Group life insurance;

2. Health insurance;

3. Disability insurance;

4. Sick leave;

5. Annual leave;

6. Educational benefits; and

7. Pensions.

f. Health Care Provider. 29 U.S.C.A. § 2611(6).

A health care provider can be:

1. A doctor of medicine or osteopathy who is authorized to practice medicine or surgery by the state in which the doctor practices or

2. Any other person determined by the Secretary of the Department of Labor (DOL) who is found to be capable of providing health care services.

g. Parent. 29 U.S.C.A. § 2611(7).

A parent is either:

1. The biological parent of an employee or

2. An individual who stood in loco parentis to an employee when the employee was his or her son or daughter.

h. Person. 29 U.S.C.A. § 2611(8).

This term is given the same meaning as under the Fair Labor Standards Act (FLSA). See 29 U.S.C.A. § 203(a). Under the FLSA, "person" means an:

1. Individual;

2. Partnership;

3. Association;

4. Corporation;

5. Business trust;

6. Legal representative; or

7. Any organized group of persons. 29 U.S.C.A. § 203(a).

i. Reduced Leave Schedule. 29 U.S.C.A. § 2611(9).

This is an employee's leave schedule that reduces his or her usual number of work hours per week or hours per day.

j. Secretary. 29 U.S.C.A. § 2611(10).

This is the Secretary of the Department of Labor (DOL).

k. Serious Health Condition. 29 U.S.C.A. § 2611(11).

A serious health condition is an illness, injury, impairment, or physical or mental condition that involves:

1. Inpatient care in a hospital, hospice, or residential medical care facility or

2. Continuing treatment by a health care provider.

l. Son or Daughter. 29 U.S.C.A. § 2611(12).

This means a:

1. Biological child;

2. Adopted child;

3. Foster child;

4. Step-child;

5. Legal ward; or

6. Child of a person standing in loco parentis.

However, any of the above must be:

1. Under eighteen years of age or

2. Eighteen years of age or older and incapable of self-care because of a mental or physical disability.

m. Spouse. 29 U.S.C.A. § 2611(13).

A husband or wife as the case may be.

3. LEAVE ENTITLEMENTS

An eligible employee is entitled to a total of twelve workweeks of leave during any twelve month period. The leave may be taken for one or more of the following reasons:

1. The birth of a daughter or son and to care for this daughter or son;

2. The placement of a daughter or son with the employee for adoption or foster care;

3. To care for the spouse, daughter, son, or parent, of the employee, if this spouse, daughter, son, or parent has a serious health condition; or

4. For a serious health condition that makes the employee unable to perform the functions of his or her position. 29 U.S.C.A. § 2612(a)(1).

The entitlement of a leave for a birth or placement of a daughter or son expires at the end of the twelve month period beginning on the date of the birth or placement.

a. Spouses Employed by the Same Employer

Where a husband and wife are employed by the same employer, the total number of workweeks of leave to which both may be entitled may be limited by the employer to twelve workweeks during any twelve month period for:

1. The birth of a daughter or son and to care for this daughter or son;

2. The placement of a daughter or son with the employee for adoption or foster care; or

3. The care of a sick parent of the employee, if this parent has a serious health condition. 29 U.S.C.A. § 2612(f).

This total twelve workweek limitation during any twelve month period for spouses employed by the same employer does not apply to an FMLA leave for:

1. Either the husband's or the wife's own leave for a serious health condition that makes the employee unable to perform the functions of his or her position or

2. The care of a spouse, daughter, or son of the employee, if this spouse, daughter, or son has a serious health condition. 29 U.S.C.A. § 2612(f).

b. Paid Leave Substitution

An employee is generally entitled to twelve weeks of unpaid FMLA leave. 29 U.S.C.A. §§ 2612(c), 2612(d)(1). However, an eligible employee may elect or an employer may require the employee to substitute any accrued paid vacation leave, paid personal leave, or paid family leave for any part of the FMLA unpaid twelve week period where this leave is for:

1. The birth of a daughter or son and to care for this daughter or son;

2. The placement of a daughter or son with the employee for adoption or foster care; or

3.　The care of a spouse, daughter, son, or parent of the employee, if this spouse, daughter, son, or parent has a serious health condition. 29 U.S.C.A. § 2612(d)(2)(A).

An eligible employee may elect or an employer may require the employee to substitute any accrued paid vacation leave, paid personal leave, paid medical leave, or paid sick leave for any part of the FMLA unpaid twelve week period where this leave is:

1.　To care for the spouse, daughter, son, or parent of the employee, if this spouse, daughter, son, or parent has a serious health condition; or

2.　For a serious health condition that makes the employee unable to perform the functions of his or her position. 29 U.S.C.A. § 2612(d)(2)(B).

The FMLA, however, does not require an employer to provide paid sick leave or paid medical leave in any situation in which the employer would normally not provide this type of paid leave. 29 U.S.C.A. § 2612(d)(2)(B).

4.　LEAVE TYPES

a.　Foreseeable Leave—Birth/Placement of a Child

An employee must provide a minimum thirty days notice before the date the FMLA leave is to begin, unless this is not practicable, for a leave involving:

1. The birth of a daughter or son and to care for this daughter or son or

2. The placement of a daughter or son with the employee for adoption or foster care. 29 U.S.C.A. § 2612(e)(1).

b. Foreseeable Leave—Planned Medical Treatment

An employee must give a minimum thirty days notice where the necessity for an FMLA leave is foreseeable based on planned medical treatment. If the date of the treatment requires leave to begin in less than thirty days, the employee must provide notice as soon as practicable. 29 U.S.C.A. § 2612(e)(2)(B). Leave for planned medical treatment may be taken:

1. To care for the spouse, daughter, son, or parent of the employee, if this spouse, daughter, son, or parent has a serious health condition; or

2. For a serious health condition that makes the employee unable to perform the functions of his or her position. 29 U.S.C.A. § 2612(e)(2).

The employee must make a reasonable effort to schedule the treatment to not disrupt unduly the employer's operations, subject to the approval of the:

1. Employee's health care provider or

2. Health care provider of the spouse, daughter, son, or parent. 29 U.S.C.A. § 2612(e)(2)(A).

c. Intermittent Leave/Reduced Leave Schedule—Generally

Certain leaves may be taken intermittently or on a reduced leave schedule by the employee. 29 U.S.C.A. § 2612(b)(1). These leaves may be taken when medically necessary:

1. To care for the spouse, daughter, son, or parent of the employee, if this spouse, daughter, son, or parent has a serious health condition or

2. For a serious health condition that makes the employee unable to perform the functions of his or her position.

Leave for a birth or placement of a daughter or son cannot be taken intermittently or on a reduced leave schedule unless the employee and the employer agree.

The taking of intermittent leave or a reduced leave schedule may not result in a reduction in the total amount of FMLA leave to which the employee was entitled beyond the amount of the leave actually taken.

d. Intermittent Leave/Reduced Leave Schedule—Alternative Position

An employer may require the employee to transfer temporarily to an available alternative position, where an employee requests intermittent leave or leave on a reduced leave schedule that is foreseeable based on planned medical treatment:

1. To care for the spouse, daughter, son, or parent of the employee, if this spouse, daughter, son, or parent has a serious health condition or

2. For a serious health condition that makes the employee unable to perform the functions of his or her position. 29 U.S.C.A. § 2612(b)(2).

The available alternative position must be one for which the employee is qualified. It must:

1. Have equivalent pay and benefits and

2. Better accommodate recurring periods of leave than the employee's regular employment position.

5. MEDICAL CERTIFICATIONS

An employer may require a certification from a health care provider to support and verify FMLA leaves:

1. To care for the spouse, daughter, son, or parent of the employee, if this spouse, daughter, son, or parent has a serious health condition; or

2. For a serious health condition that makes the employee unable to perform the functions of his or her position. 29 U.S.C.A. § 2613(a).

This certification may be required from the health care provider of the:

1. Eligible employee or

2. Spouse, daughter, son, or parent.

The employee must provide a copy of this certification in a timely manner. 29 U.S.C.A. § 2613(a).

a. Medical Certification—Employee's Care of Spouse, Daughter, Son, or Parent with a Serious Health Condition

To care for a spouse, daughter, son, or parent of the employee, if this spouse, daughter, son, or parent has a serious health condition, the certification must include:

1. The date on which the serious health condition commenced;

2. The condition's probable duration;

3. The appropriate medical facts within the health care provider's knowledge regarding the condition;

4. A statement that the employee is needed to care for the spouse, daughter, son, or parent; and

5. An estimate of the amount of time that the employee is needed to care for the spouse, daughter, son, or parent. 29 U.S.C.A. § 2613(b)(4)(A).

b. Medical Certification—Employee's Serious Health Condition

For a serious health condition that makes the employee unable to perform the functions of his or her position, the employee's certification must include:

1. The date on which the serious health condition commenced;

2. The condition's probable duration;

3. The appropriate medical facts within the health care provider's knowledge regarding the condition; and

4. A statement that the employee is unable to perform the functions of the position for which he or she is employed. 29 U.S.C.A. § 2613(b)(4)(B).

c. Medical Certification—Intermittent Leave/ Reduced Leave Schedule—Employee's Care of Spouse, Daughter, Son, or Parent with a Serious Health Condition

To care for a spouse, daughter, son, or parent of the employee, if this spouse, daughter, son, or parent has a serious health condition, the certification for intermittent leave or leave on a reduced leave schedule must include a statement indicating:

1. That the employee is needed to care for the spouse, daughter, son, or parent who has a serious health condition or will assist in their recovery and

2. The intermittent leave's or reduced leave schedule's expected duration and schedule. 29 U.S.C.A. § 2613(b)(7).

d. Medical Certification—Intermittent Leave/ Reduced Leave Schedule—Employee's Planned Medical Treatment

Where an employee takes intermittent leave or leave on a reduced leave schedule for planned medical treatment, the employee is required to provide a certification containing:

1. The dates on which the treatment is expected to be given and

2. The treatment's duration. 29 U.S.C.A. § 2613(b)(5).

e. Medical Certification—Intermittent Leave/Reduced Leave Schedule—Employee's Serious Health Condition

For a serious health condition that makes the employee unable to perform the functions of his or her position, the employee's certification for intermittent leave or leave on a reduced schedule must include a statement of:

1. The medical necessity for the leave and

2. The leave's expected duration. 29 U.S.C.A. § 2613(b)(6).

f. Medical Certification—Second Opinion

An employer may require a second opinion from a second health care provider where the employer has reason to doubt the original certification's validity where the employee's FMLA leave is:

1. To care for the spouse, daughter, son, or parent of the employee, if this spouse, daughter, son, or parent has a serious health condition; or

2. For a serious health condition that makes the employee unable to perform the functions of his or her position. 29 U.S.C.A. § 2613(c)(1).

In securing the second opinion, the employer is entitled to information relating to:

1. The date on which the serious health condition commenced;

2. The condition's probable duration; and

3. The appropriate medical facts within the health care provider's knowledge regarding the condition.

The employer must pay the employee's expense in securing the second opinion. However, the employer may designate the second health care provider or approve the employee's choice of the second health care provider. In neither case, shall the health care provider who is engaged to provide the second opinion be employed on a regular basis by the employer.

Where the second opinion differs from the original certification, the employer may require, at the employer's expense, that the employee obtain a third health care provider's opinion. The third health care provider must be designated or approved jointly by the employee and the employer and must provide information regarding:

1. The date on which the serious health condition commenced;

2. The condition's probable duration; and

3. The appropriate medical facts within the health care provider's knowledge regarding the condition. 29 U.S.C.A. § 2613(d).

Where a third opinion is required, it is considered final and binding on the employee and the employer.

g. Medical Certification—Subsequent Recertification

The employer may require that the employee obtain subsequent recertifications on a reasonable basis. 29 U.S.C.A. § 2613(e).

h. Medical Certification Prior to Position Restoration

For an FMLA leave for a serious health condition that makes the employee unable to perform the functions of his or her position, the employer may require a medical certification prior to restoration of the employee's position. This certification can only be required by the employer where the employer has a uniformly applied practice or policy that requires each employee to receive a certification from the employee's health care provider that the employee is able to resume work. However, this part of the FMLA does not supersede a valid state or local law or a collective bargaining agreement that governs the employee's return to work. 29 U.S.C.A. § 2614(a)(4).

i. Medical Certification—Failure to Return to Work

An employer can require a medical certification where the employee is unable to return to work because of the continuation, recurrence, or onset of a serious health condition:

1. To care for the spouse, daughter, son, or parent of the employee, if this spouse, daughter, son, or parent has a serious health condition or

2. For a serious health condition that makes the employee unable to perform the functions of his or her position. 29 U.S.C.A. § 2614(c)(3)(A).

The employee must provide a timely copy of the certification and it must be supported by the following:

1. A certification issued by the health care provider of the spouse, daughter, son, or parent of the employee, as appropriate or

2. A certification by the health care provider of the eligible employee, in the case of an employee unable to return to work. 29 U.S.C.A. § 2614(c)(3)(A).

The certification will be deemed to be sufficient if it states that:

1. The employee is needed to care for the spouse, daughter, son, or parent who has a serious health condition on the date that the employee's FMLA expires or

2. A serious health condition prevented the employee from being able to perform the functions of the employee's position on the date that the employee's FMLA expired. 29 U.S.C.A. § 2614(c)(3)(C).

When this occurs, the employer cannot recover the cost of the health care benefits provided to the employee while on leave. 29 U.S.C.A. § 2614(c)(2)(B).

6. BENEFIT PROTECTION WHILE ON LEAVE

During any FMLA leave, the employer is required to maintain the group health plan coverage for the entire leave period. 29 U.S.C.A. § 2614(c)(1). The taking of any FMLA leave cannot result in the loss of any employment benefit that was accrued prior to the date on which the leave commenced. 29 U.S.C.A. § 2614(a)(2).

7. COST OF MAINTAINING HEALTH CARE COVERAGE

The employer may recover the cost for maintaining coverage for the employee under the group health plan where:

1. The employee fails to return from the leave after any period of leave has expired or

2. The employee fails to return to work for a reason other than the continuation, recurrence, or onset of a serious health condition involving:

   a. Care for the spouse, daughter, son, or parent of the employee, if this spouse, daughter, son, or parent has a serious health condition or

b.   For a serious health condition that makes the employee unable to perform the functions of his or her position.

3.   Other circumstances beyond the employee's control. 29 U.S.C.A. § 2614(c)(2)(B).

However, where the employee provides a medical certification verifying the he or she cannot return to work, the employer cannot recover the cost of these group health care benefits. 29 U.S.C.A. § 2614(c)(3)(A).

8.   RESTORATION TO POSITION

Except for certain highly compensated employees, any eligible employee who takes an FMLA leave is entitled on return from the leave to be restored by the employer to:

1.   The position of the employment held by the employee when the leave originally commenced or

2.   An equivalent position with the equivalent employment benefits, pay, and other terms and conditions of employment. 29 U.S.C.A. § 2614(a)(1).

However, an employee who is restored to his or position upon completing an FMLA leave is not entitled to:

1.   The accrual of any seniority or employment benefits during any period of leave and

2.   Any right, benefit, or position of employment other than any right, benefit, or position to

which the employee would have been entitled had the employee not taken the leave. 29 U.S.C.A. § 2614(3).

a.　Highly Compensated Employee Exemption

An employer may deny restoration to the employee's former position or to an equivalent position where the employee is a highly compensated employee. A highly compensated employee is considered to be a salaried eligible employee who is among the highest paid ten percent of the employees employed by the employer within seventy-five miles of the facility at which the employee is employed. 29 U.S.C.A. § 2614(b)(2).

Employer denial may occur when:

1.　It is necessary to prevent substantial and grievous economic injury to the employer's operations;

2.　The employer notified the employee of the employer's intent to deny restoration on this basis at the time the employer determined that this injury would occur; and

3.　The leave has commenced and the employee elects not to return to employment after receiving this notice. 29 U.S.C.A. § 2614(b)(1).

b.　Periodic Reporting

While on any FMLA leave, an employer can require an employee to report periodically on the employee's status and intention to return to work. 29 U.S.C.A. § 2614(a)(5).

c. Medical Certification Prior to Position Restoration

For an FMLA leave for a serious health condition that makes the employee unable to perform the functions of his or her position, the employer may require a medical certification prior to restoration of the employee's position. This certification can only be required by the employer where the employer has a uniformly applied practice or policy that requires each employee to receive a certification from the employee's health care provider that the employee is able to resume to work. However, this part of the FMLA does not supersede a valid state or local law or a collective bargaining agreement that governs the employee's return to work. 29 U.S.C.A. § 2614(a)(4).

d. Medical Certification—Failure to Return to Work

An employer can require a medical certification where the employee is unable to return to work because of the continuation, recurrence, or onset of a serious health condition:

1. To care for the spouse, daughter, son, or parent of the employee, if this spouse, daughter, son, or parent has a serious health condition or

2. For a serious health condition that makes the employee unable to perform the functions of

his or her position. 29 U.S.C.A. § 2614(c)(3)(A).

The employee must provide a timely copy of the certification and it must be supported by the following:

1. A certification issued by the health care provider of the daughter, son, spouse, or parent of the employee, as appropriate or

2. A certification by the health care provider of the eligible employee, in the case of an employee unable to return to work. 29 U.S.C.A. § 2614(c)(3)(A).

The certification will be deemed to be sufficient if it states that:

1. The employee is needed to care for the spouse, daughter, son, or parent who has a serious health condition on the date that the employee's FMLA leave expires or

2. A serious health condition prevented the employee from being able to perform the functions of the employee's position on the date that the employee's FMLA leave expired. 29 U.S.C.A. § 2614(c)(3)(C).

When this occurs, the employer cannot recover the cost of the health care benefits provided to the employee while on leave. 29 U.S.C.A. § 2614(c)(2)(B).

9.   SPECIAL RULES CONCERNING EMPLOYEES OF LOCAL EDU-CATION AGENCIES

Full FMLA leave privileges apply to:

1.   Any local educational agency as defined in the Elementary and Secondary Education Act of 1965 as amended by the Improving America's School Act of 1994 [20 U.S.C.A. § 2891(12), *repealed by*, 20 U.S.C.A. § 8801(18)] as an employer and an eligible employee of that employer and

2.   Any private elementary or secondary school as an employer and eligible employee of that employer.   29   U.S.C.A.   §§ 2618(a)(1), 2618(a)(2).

Under the Elementary and Secondary Education Act of 1965 as amended by the Improving America's School Act of 1994, a "local education agency" means a public board of education or other public authority legally constituted within a state for either administrative control or direction of, or to perform a service function for public elementary or secondary schools:

1.   In a county, city, township, school district, or other political subdivision of a state or

2.   For the combination of school districts or counties as are recognized in a state as an administrative agency for its public elementary or secondary schools.   20   U.S.C.A.

§ 2891(12), *repealed by*, 20 U.S.C.A. § 8801(18).

The term includes:

1. Any other public institution or agency having administrative control and direction of a public elementary or secondary school and

2. An elementary or secondary school funded by the Bureau of Indian Affairs, but only to the extent that the inclusion makes this school eligible for programs for which specific eligibility is not provided to this school in another provision of law and this school does not have a student population that is smaller than the student population of the local educational agency receiving assistance under this Act with the smallest student population, except that this school shall not be subject to the jurisdiction of any state educational agency other than the Bureau of Indian Affairs. 20 U.S.C.A. § 2891(12), *repealed by*, 20 U.S.C.A. § 8801(18).

a. Leave Does Not Violate Certain Other Federal Laws

A local educational agency and a private elementary or secondary school, solely as a result of an eligible employee exercising his or her FMLA rights, shall not be in violation of the:

1. Individuals with Disabilities Education Act [20 U.S.C.A. §§ 1400 et seq.];

2. Rehabilitation Act of 1973 [29 U.S.C.A. § 794]; or

3. Civil Rights Act of 1964 (Title VII) [29 U.S.C.A. § 2000d]. 29 U.S.C.A. § 2618(b).

b. Intermittent Leave or Leave on a Reduced Schedule for Instructional Employees

Special rules apply where an eligible employee is employed principally in an instructional capacity by an educational agency or school requests an intermittent leave or leave on a reduced schedule:

1. To care for the spouse, daughter, son, or parent of the employee, if this spouse, daughter, son, or parent has a serious health condition or

2. For a serious health condition that makes the employee unable to perform the functions of his or her position. 29 U.S.C.A. § 2618(c).

Where this leave is foreseeable based on planned medical treatment and the employee would be on leave for greater than twenty percent of the total number of working days in the period during which the leave would extend, the educational agency or school may require the employee to elect either:

1. To take the leave for period of a particular duration not to exceed the duration of the planned medical treatment or

2. To transfer temporarily to an available alternative position offered by the employer for which the employee is qualified, and that:

a. Has equivalent pay and benefits and

b. Better accommodates recurring periods of leave than the regular employment position of the employee. 29 U.S.C.A. § 2618(c).

This election only applies to an employee who complies with the FMLA's requirements for foreseeable leave. 29 U.S.C.A. § 2618(c)(2). The employee must give notice where the necessity for an FMLA leave is foreseeable based on planned medical treatment:

1. To care for the spouse, daughter, son, or parent of the employee, if this spouse, daughter, son, or parent has a serious health condition or

2. For a serious health condition that makes the employee unable to perform the functions of his or her position. 29 U.S.C.A. § 2612(e)(2).

In these cases, the employee must make a reasonable effort to schedule the treatment to not disrupt unduly the employer's operations, subject to the approval of the:

1. Employee's health care provider or

2. Health care provider of the spouse, daughter, son, or parent. 29 U.S.C.A. § 2612(e)(2)(A).

The employee must provide the employer with not less than thirty days' notice before the date the leave is to begin of the employee's intention to take this leave. If the date of the treatment requires leave to begin in less than thirty days, the employee must provide notice as soon as practicable. 29 U.S.C.A. § 2612(e)(2)(B).

c. Rules Applicable to Periods Near the Conclusion of an Academic Term

The following rules apply with respect to periods of FMLA leave near the conclusion of an academic term where an employee is employed primarily in an instructional capacity by the educational agency or school:

1. *Leave More than Five Weeks Prior to the End of the Term.* If the employee begins any FMLA leave more than five weeks prior to the academic term's end, the educational agency or school may require the employee to continue taking the leave until the term's end, if:

   a. The leave is of at least three weeks duration and

   b. The return to employment would occur during the three week period before the term's end. 29 U.S.C.A. § 2618(d)(1).

2. *Leave Less than Five Weeks Prior to the End of the Term.* Special rules apply if the employee begins a leave:

   a. For the birth of a daughter or son and to care for this daughter or son;

   b. For the placement of a daughter or son with the employee for adoption or foster care; or

   c. To care for the spouse, daughter, son, or parent of the employee, if this spouse, daughter, son, or parent has a serious health condition.

If these leaves commence five weeks prior to academic term's end, the educational agency or the school may require the employee to continue taking the leave until the term's end, if:

   a. The leave is of greater than two weeks duration and

   b. The return to employment would occur during the two week period before the term's end. 29 U.S.C.A. § 2618(d)(2).

  3. *Leave Less than Three Weeks Prior to the Term's End.* Special rules apply if the employee begins a leave:

   a. For the birth of a daughter or son and to care for this daughter or son;

   b. For the placement of a daughter or son with the employee for adoption or foster care; or

   c. To care for the spouse, daughter, son, or parent of the employee, if this spouse, daughter, son, or parent has a serious health condition.

If these leaves commence three weeks prior to academic term's end, the educational agency or the school may require the employee to continue to take the leave until the term's end. 29 U.S.C.A. § 2618(d)(3).

d. Restoration of Equivalent Employment Position

Upon completion of any FMLA leave, restoration to the same or equivalent employment position is required to be made by an educational agency or a private elementary or secondary school on the basis of established school board policies and practices, private school policies and practices, and collective bargaining agreements. 29 U.S.C.A. § 2618(e).

e. Reduction of the Amount of Liability for FMLA Violations

If a local educational agency or a private elementary or secondary school that has violated the FMLA proves to the court's satisfaction that the agency, school, or department had reasonable grounds for believing that the underlying act or omission was not an FMLA violation, the court may, in its discretion, reduce the amount of liability to the amount and interest actually due without assessing the full amount or any liquidated damages. 29 U.S.C.A. § 2618(e).

10.   EMPLOYER FMLA NOTICE

Every employer is required to post and keep posted, in conspicuous places on the employer's premises where applicant and employee notices are customarily posted, an FMLA notice, to be prepared or approved by the Secretary of Labor. This notice must set forth excerpts from, or summaries of:

1.   The FMLA's pertinent provisions and

2. Information relating to filing complaints.

An employer who willfully violates this posting requirement may be assessed a civil money penalty not to exceed $100.00 for each separate offense. 29 U.S.C.A. § 2619.

11. EMPLOYER RECORDKEEPING

An employer is required to keep and preserve records pertaining to compliance with the FMLA in accordance with the Fair Labor Standards Act's (FLSA's) [29 U.S.C.A. § 211(c)] recordkeeping requirements and in accordance with regulations issued by the Secretary of Labor. 29 U.S.C.A. § 2616(b). Under the FLSA, the Secretary of Labor may require an employer through regulations or for enforcement purposes to:

1. Make, keep, and preserve any records of the persons employed relating to these persons wages, hours, and other conditions and practices of employment;

2. Preserve these records for the prescribed time periods; and

3. Provide reports. 29 U.S.C.A. § 211(c).

The Secretary of Labor cannot require any employer or any plan, fund, or program to submit to the Secretary any books or records more than once during any twelve month period unless the Secretary has reasonable cause to believe that there may exist a violation of the FMLA or its regulations. 29 U.S.C.A. § 2616(c).

12. PROHIBITED EMPLOYER ACTS

The FMLA prohibits employers from:

1. Interfering with, restraining, or denying the exercise of or the attempt to exercise, any right provided under the FMLA by an employee;

2. Terminating or in any other manner discriminating against any individual for opposing any practice made unlawful by the FMLA; and

3. Terminating or in any manner discriminating against any individual because the individual has:

   a. Filed any charge or has instituted or caused to be instituted any proceeding under or related to the FMLA;

   b. Given or is about to give any information in connection with any inquiry or proceeding relating to any right provided under the FMLA; or

   c. Testified or is about to testify in any inquiry or proceeding relating to any right provided under the FMLA. 29 U.S.C.A. § 2615.

13. FMLA ENFORCEMENT AND REMEDIES FOR VIOLATIONS

a. Investigative Authority

To ensure compliance with the FMLA's provisions, the Secretary of Labor has the same investigative authority as that contained in the Fair Labor Standards Act (FLSA) [29 U.S.C.A. § 211(a)]. 29 U.S.C.A. § 2616(a). Under the FLSA, the Secretary of Labor or his or her designated representative may investigate and gather data regarding wages, hours, and other conditions and practices of employment. This investigation includes:

1.   Entering and inspecting places and records;

2.   Making transcriptions of records;

3.   Questioning employees; and

4.   Reviewing facts, conditions, practices, or matters as may be deemed necessary or appropriate to determine:

    a.   Whether any violation has been committed or

    b.   Enforcement. 29 U.S.C.A. § 211(a).

b. Subpoena Powers

Under the FMLA, the Secretary of Labor is given the same subpoena authority as under the Fair Labor Standards Act (FLSA) [29 U.S.C.A. § 209]. 29 U.S.C.A. § 2616(d). Under the FLSA, the Secretary of Labor can for any hearing or investigation require the:

1.   Attendance of witnesses and

2.   Production of books, paper, and documents. 29 U.S.C.A. § 209.

c. Statute of Limitations for FMLA Claims— Nonwillful Violations

Except for a willful FMLA violation, an action may be brought not later than two years after the date of the last event constituting the alleged violation for which the action is brought has occurred. 29 U.S.C.A. § 2617(c)(1).

d. Statute of Limitations for FMLA Claims— Willful Violations

For a willful FMLA violation, an action must be brought not later than three years after the date of the last event constituting the alleged violation for which the action is brought has occurred. 29 U.S.C.A. § 2617(c)(2).

e. Right of Action—Employees

An action to recover damages or equitable relief may be maintained against any employer, including a public agency, in any federal or state court of competent jurisdiction by any one or more employees for and in behalf of:

1. The employees or

2. The employees and other employees similarly situated. 29 U.S.C.A. § 2617(a)(2).

However, this right to bring an action by or on behalf of any employee shall terminate:

1. On the filing of a complaint by the Secretary of Labor for recovery of the damages sought that are owing to an employee for an employ-

er's FMLA violation, unless the action is dismissed without prejudice on motion of the Secretary or

2. On the filing of a complaint by the Secretary of Labor for injunctive relief to restrain any further delay in the payment of the damages found to be owed to the employee by an employer responsible for an FMLA violation. 29 U.S.C.A. § 2617(a)(4).

f. Secretary of Labor—Administrative Actions

The Secretary of Labor shall receive, investigate, and attempt to resolve complaints where an employer:

1. Interferes with, restrains, or denies the exercise of or the attempt to exercise, any right provided under the FMLA by an employee;

2. Terminates or in any other manner discriminates against any individual for opposing any practice made unlawful by the FMLA; and

3. Terminates or in any manner discriminates against any individual because the individual has:

   a. Filed any charge or has instituted or caused to be instituted any proceeding under or related to the FMLA;

   b. Given or is about to give any information in connection with any inquiry or proceeding

relating to any right provided under the
FMLA; or

c. Testified or is about to testify in any inquiry or proceeding relating to any right provided under the FMLA. 29 U.S.C.A.
§§ 2615, 2617(b)(1).

The Secretary of Labor must receive, investigate,
and attempt to resolve these complaints in the same
manner as it does minimum wage and overtime
violations under the Fair Labor Standards Act
(FLSA) [29 U.S.C.A. §§ 206, 207]. 29 U.S.C.A.
§ 2617(b)(1).

g. Secretary of Labor—Civil Actions

The Secretary of Labor may bring an action in
any court of competent jurisdiction to recover damages for:

1. *General Damages.* Damages equal to the
   amount of any wages, salary, employment
   benefits, or other compensation denied or lost
   to the employee by reason of violating the
   FMLA plus:

   a. Interest. The interest on this amount calcu-
      lated at the prevailing rate and

   b. Liquidated Damages. An additional amount
      as liquidated damages equal to the sum of
      the amount permitted as damages and in-
      terest unless the employer can prove to the
      court's satisfaction that the act or omission
      that caused the FMLA violation was in
      good faith and that the employer had rea-

sonable grounds for believing that the act or omission was not an FMLA violation and the court may, in its discretion, reduce the liability for the liquidated damages amount to the amount permitted as damages and interest.

2. *Actual Monetary Loss.* In a case where wages, salary, employment benefits, or other compensation have not been denied or lost to the employee, any actual monetary losses sustained by the employee as a direct result of the violation, for example, the cost of providing care, up to a sum equal to twelve weeks of wages for the employee. 29 U.S.C.A. §§ 2617(a)(1), 2617(b)(2).

Any damages recovered by the Secretary of Labor are to be held in a special deposit account and shall be paid, on order of the Secretary, directly to each employee affected. Any damages not paid to an employee because of an inability to do so within a three year period from their recovery shall be deposited into the United States Treasury. 29 U.S.C.A. § 2617(b)(3).

h. Commencement of Actions by Secretary of Labor

In determining when an action is commenced by the Secretary of Labor, it shall be considered to be commenced on the date when the complaint is filed. 29 U.S.C.A. § 2617(c)(3).

i. Injunctions by the Secretary of Labor

United States District Courts are given jurisdiction, for cause shown, to issue injunctive relief in an action brought by the Secretary of Labor to:

1. Restrain, interfere with, deny the exercise of, or the attempt to exercise any right provided under the FMLA by an employee;

2. Restrain, terminate, or in any other manner discriminate against any individual for opposing any practice made unlawful by the FMLA;

3. Restrain, terminate, or in any manner discriminate against any individual because the individual has:

    a. Filed any charge or has instituted or caused to be instituted any proceeding under or related to the FMLA;

    b. Given or is about to give any information in connection with any inquiry or proceeding relating to any right provided under the FMLA; or

    c. Testified or is about to testify in any inquiry or proceeding relating to any right provided under the FMLA.

4. Restrain the withholding of the payment of wages, salary, employment benefits, or other compensation, plus interest, found by the court to be due to the employee; and

5. Award any other equitable relief as may be appropriate, including employment, reinstate-

ment, and promotion. 29 U.S.C.A. §§ 2615, 2617(d).

j. Solicitor of Labor

The Solicitor of Labor may appear for and represent the Secretary of Labor in any FMLA litigation. 29 U.S.C.A. § 2617(e).

k. Employer Liability

Any employer who violates the FMLA shall be liable for:

1. *General Damages.* Damages equal to the amount of any wages, salary, employment benefits, or other compensation denied or lost to the employee by reason of the FMLA violation plus:

    a. Interest. The interest on this amount calculated at the prevailing rate and

    b. Liquidated Damages. An additional amount as liquidated damages equal to the sum of the amount permitted as damages and interest unless the employer can prove to the court's satisfaction that the act or omission that caused the FMLA violation was in good faith and that the employer had reasonable grounds for believing that the act or omission was not an FMLA violation and the court may, in its discretion, reduce the liability for the liquidated damages amount to the amount permitted as damages and interest.

2. *Actual Monetary Loss.* In a case where wages, salary, employment benefits, or other compensation have not been denied or lost to the employee, any actual monetary losses sustained by the employee as a direct result of the violation, for example, the cost of providing care, up to a sum equal to twelve weeks of wages for the employee.

3. *Equitable Relief.* Any equitable relief that the court may find appropriate. 29 U.S.C.A. § 2617(a)(1).

4. *Attorney's Fee, Expert Witness Fee, Costs, etc.* The court in any action where the plaintiff is awarded a judgment must allow a reasonable attorney's fee, reasonable expert witness fee, and other costs of the action to be paid by the defendant. 29 U.S.C.A. § 2617(a)(3).

l. Reduction of the Amount of Liability—Employees of Local Educational Agencies

If a local educational agency or a private elementary or secondary school that has violated the FMLA proves to the court's satisfaction that the agency, school, or department had reasonable grounds for believing that the underlying act or omission was not a violation of the FMLA, the court may, in its discretion, reduce the amount of liability to the amount and interest actually due without assessing the full amount or any liquidated damages. 29 U.S.C.A. § 2618(e).

D. TITLE II—LEAVE FOR FEDERAL CIVIL SERVICE EMPLOYEES

1. TITLE II—GENERALLY

The FMLA's Title II provides the same type of information as Title I but covers federal civil service employees. 5 U.S.C.A. §§ 6381–6387.

2. DEFINITIONS

a. Employee. 5 U.S.C.A. § 6381(1).

An employee is any individual that:

1. Is an "employee" as defined by the FMLA's Section 6301(2), including any individual employed in a position referred to in clause (v) or (ix), but excluding any individual employed by the government of the District of Columbia and any individual employed on a temporary or intermittent basis and

2. Has completed at least twelve months of service.

b. Health Care Provider. 5 U.S.C.A. § 6381(2).

Health care provider means:

1. A doctor of medicine or osteopathy who is authorized to practice medicine or surgery by the state in which the doctor practices and

2. Any other person determined by the Director of the Office of Personnel Management to be capable of providing health care services.

c. Parent. 5 U.S.C.A. § 6381(3).

A parent is either:

1. The biological parent of an employee or

2. An individual who stood in loco parentis to an employee when the employee was his or her son or daughter.

d. Reduced Leave Schedule. 5 U.S.C.A. § 6381(4).

An employee's leave schedule that reduces his or her usual number of hours per workweek or hours per workday.

e. Serious Health Condition. 5 U.S.C.A. § 6381(5).

A serious health condition is an illness, injury, impairment, or physical or mental condition that involves:

1. Inpatient care in a hospital, hospice, or residential medical care facility or

2. Continuing treatment by a health care provider.

f. Son or Daughter. 5 U.S.C.A. § 6381(6).

This means a:

1. Biological child;

2. Adopted child;

3. Foster child;

4. Step-child;

5. Legal ward; or

6. Child of a person standing in loco parentis.

However, any of the above must be:

1. Under eighteen years of age or

2. Eighteen years of age or older and incapable of self-care because of a mental or physical disability.

3. LEAVE ENTITLEMENTS

a. Leave Entitlement—Generally

An eligible employee is entitled to a total of twelve workweeks of leave during any twelve month period. The leave may be taken for one or more of the following reasons:

1. The birth of a daughter or son and to care for this daughter or son;

2. The placement of a daughter or son with the employee for adoption or foster care;

3. To care for the spouse, daughter, son, or parent of the employee, if this spouse, daughter, son, or parent has a serious health condition; or

4. For a serious health condition that makes the employee unable to perform the functions of his or her position. 5 U.S.C.A. § 6382(a)(1).

However, the entitlement of a leave for a birth or placement of a daughter or son expires at the end of the twelve month period beginning on the date of the birth or placement.

b. Paid Leave Substitution

An employee is generally entitled to twelve weeks of unpaid FMLA leave. 5 U.S.C.A. §§ 6382(a)(1), 6382(c). However, an eligible employee may elect to substitute any accrued or accumulated paid annual leave or paid sick leave for any part of the FMLA unpaid twelve week period where this leave is for:

1. The birth of a daughter or son and to care for this daughter or son;

2. The placement of a daughter or son with the employee for adoption or foster care;

3. To care for the spouse, daughter, son, or parent of the employee, if this spouse, daughter, son, or parent has a serious health condition; or

4. For a serious health condition that makes the employee unable to perform the functions of his or her position. 5 U.S.C.A. § 6382(d).

The FMLA, however, does not require an employer to provide paid sick leave in any situation in which the employer would normally not provide this type of paid leave. 5 U.S.C.A. § 6382(d).

4. LEAVE TYPES

a. Foreseeable Leave—Birth/Placement of a Child

An employee must provide a minimum thirty days' notice before the date the FMLA leave is to begin, unless this is not practicable, for a leave involving:

1. The birth of a daughter or son and to care for this daughter or son or

2. The placement of a daughter or son with the employee for adoption or foster care. 5 U.S.C.A. § 6382(e)(1).

b. Foreseeable Leave—Planned Medical Treatment

An employee must give notice where the necessity for an FMLA leave is foreseeable based on planned medical treatment:

1. To care for the spouse, daughter, son, or parent of the employee, if this spouse, daughter, son, or parent has a serious health condition or

2. For a serious health condition that makes the employee unable to perform the functions of his or her position. 5 U.S.C.A. § 6382(e)(2).

In these cases, the employee must make a reasonable effort to schedule the treatment to not disrupt unduly the employer's operations, subject to the approval of the:

1. Employee's health care provider or

2. Health care provider of the spouse, daughter, son, or parent. 5 U.S.C.A. § 6382(e)(2)(A).

The employee must provide the employer with not less than thirty days' notice before the date the leave is to begin of the employee's intention to take this leave. If the date of the treatment requires leave to begin in less than thirty days, the employee must provide notice as soon as practicable. 5 U.S.C.A. § 6382(e)(2)(B).

c. Intermittent Leave/Reduced Leave Schedule—Generally

Certain leaves may be taken intermittently or on a reduced leave schedule by the employee. 5 U.S.C.A. § 6382(b)(1). These leaves may be taken when medically necessary:

1. To care for the spouse, daughter, son, or parent of the employee, if this spouse, daughter, son, or parent has a serious health condition or

2. For a serious health condition that makes the employee unable to perform the functions of his or her position.

Leave for a birth or placement of a daughter or son cannot be taken intermittently or on a reduced leave schedule unless the employee and the employer agree.

The taking of intermittent leave or a reduced leave schedule may not result in a reduction in the total amount of FMLA leave to which the employee was entitled beyond the amount of the leave actually taken. Any hours of leave so taken by the employee must be subtracted from the total amount of leave remaining available to the employee on an hour-for-hour basis.

d. Intermittent Leave/Reduced Leave Schedule—Alternative Position

An employer may require the employee to transfer temporarily to an available alternative position, where an employee requests intermittent leave or leave on a reduced leave schedule that is foreseeable based on planned medical treatment:

1. To care for the spouse, daughter, son, or parent of the employee, if this spouse, daughter, son, or parent has a serious health condition or

2. For a serious health condition that makes the employee unable to perform the functions of his or her position. 5 U.S.C.A. § 6382(b)(2).

The available alternative position must be one for which the employee is qualified. The alternative position must:

1. Have equivalent pay and benefits and

2. Better accommodate recurring periods of leave than the employee's regular employment position.

5. MEDICAL CERTIFICATION

An employer may require a medical certification from a health care provider to support and verify FMLA leaves:

1. To care for the spouse, daughter, son, or parent of the employee, if this spouse, daughter, son, or parent has a serious health condition or

2. For a serious health condition that makes the employee unable to perform the functions of his or her position. 5 U.S.C.A. § 6383(a).

This certification may be required from the health care provider of the:

1. Eligible employee or

2. Spouse, daughter, son, or parent.

The employee must provide a copy of this certification in a timely manner. A certification is generally sufficient if it states:

1. The date on which the serious health condition commenced;

2. The condition's probable duration; and

3. The appropriate medical facts within the health care provider's knowledge regarding the condition. 5 U.S.C.A. § 6383(b).

a. Medical Certification—Employee's Care of Spouse, Daughter, Son, or Parent

To care for a spouse, daughter, son, or parent of the employee, if this spouse, daughter, son, or parent has a serious health condition, the certification must include:

1. The date on which the serious health condition commenced;

2. The condition's probable duration;

3. The appropriate medical facts within the health care provider's knowledge regarding the condition;

4. A statement that the employee is needed to care for the spouse, daughter, son, or parent; and

5. An estimate of the amount of time that the employee is needed to care for the spouse, daughter, son, or parent. 5 U.S.C.A. § 6383(b)(4)(A).

b. Medical Certification—Employee's Serious Health Condition

For a serious health condition that makes the employee unable to perform the functions of his or her position, the employee's certification must include:

1. The date on which the serious health condition commenced;

2. The condition's probable duration;

3. The appropriate medical facts within the health care provider's knowledge regarding the condition; and

4. A statement that the employee is unable to perform the functions of the position for which he or she is employed. 5 U.S.C.A. § 6383(b)(4)(B).

c. Medical Certification—Intermittent Leave/Reduced Leave Schedule—Planned Medical Treatment

Where an employee takes intermittent leave or leave on a reduced leave schedule for planned medical treatment, the employee is required to provide the dates on which the treatment is expected to be given and the duration of the treatment. 5 U.S.C.A. § 6383(b)(5).

d. Medical Certification—Second Opinion

An employer may require a second opinion from a second health care provider where the employer has reason to doubt the original certification's validity where the employee's FMLA leave is:

1. To care for the spouse, daughter, son, or parent of the employee, if this spouse, daughter, son, or parent has a serious health condition or

2. For a serious health condition that makes the employee unable to perform the functions of his or her position. 5 U.S.C.A. § 6383(c)(1).

In securing the second opinion, the employer is entitled to information relating to:

1. The date on which the serious health condition commenced;

2. The condition's probable duration; and

3. The appropriate medical facts within the health care provider's knowledge regarding the condition.

The employer must pay the employee's expense in securing the second opinion. However, the employer may designate the second health care provider or approve the employee's choice of the second health care provider. In neither case, shall the health care provider who is engaged to provide the second opinion be employed on a regular basis by the employer.

Where the second opinion differs from the original certification's opinion, the employer may require, at the employer's expense, that the employee obtain a third health care provider's opinion. The third health care provider must be designated or approved jointly by the employee and the employer and must provide information regarding:

1. The date on which the serious health condition commenced;

2. The condition's probable duration; and

3. The appropriate medical facts within the health care provider's knowledge regarding the condition. 5 U.S.C.A. § 6383(d)(2).

Where a third opinion is required, it shall be considered to be final and binding on the employee and the employer

e. Medical Certification—Subsequent Recertification

The employer may require that the employee obtain subsequent recertifications on a reasonable basis at the employer's cost. 5 U.S.C.A. § 6383(e).

6. BENEFIT PROTECTION WHILE ON LEAVE

The taking of any FMLA leave cannot result in the loss of any employment benefit that was accrued prior to the date on which the leave com-

menced. 5 U.S.C.A. § 6384(b). An employee enrolled
in a health benefits plan who is placed in an FMLA
leave status may elect to continue the health benefits enrollment of the employee while on this leave
and arrange to pay currently into the Employees
Health Benefits Fund the appropriate employee
contributions. 5 U.S.C.A. § 6386.

7.   RESTORATION TO POSITION

Any eligible employee who takes any type of
FMLA leave is entitled on return from the leave to
be:

1.   Restored by the employer to the position of
     the employment held by the employee when
     the leave commenced or

2.   Restored to an equivalent position with the
     equivalent employment benefits, pay, status,
     and other terms and conditions of employ-
     ment. 5 U.S.C.A. § 6384(a).

However, an employee who is restored to his or
position upon completing an FMLA leave is not
entitled to:

1.   The accrual of any employment benefits dur-
     ing any period of leave or

2.   Any right, benefit, or position of employment
     other than any right, benefit, or position to
     which the employee would have been entitled
     had the employee not taken the leave. 5
     U.S.C.A. § 6384(c).

a. Medical Certification—Restoration of Position

For an FMLA leave for a serious health condition that makes the employee unable to perform the functions of his or her position, the employer may require a medical certification prior to restoration of the employee's position. This certification can only be required by the employer where the employer has a uniformly applied practice or policy that requires each employee to receive a certification from a health care provider of the employee that the employee is able to resume to work. 5 U.S.C.A. § 6384(d).

b. Periodic Reporting

While on any FMLA leave, an employer can require an employee to report periodically on the employee's status and intention to return to work. 5 U.S.C.A. § 6384(e).

8. PROHIBITED EMPLOYEE ACTS

An employee shall not directly or indirectly intimidate, threaten, or coerce, or attempt to intimidate, threaten, or coerce, any other employee for the purpose of interfering with the exercise of any FMLA rights which the other employee may have. Intimidate, threaten, or coerce includes:

1. Promising to confer or conferring any benefit, including appointment, promotion, or compensation, or

2. Taking or threatening to take any reprisal, including deprivation of appointment, promotion, or compensation. 5 U.S.C.A. § 6385.

9. REGULATIONS

The Office of Personnel Management is responsible for prescribing regulations. These regulations shall, to the extent appropriate, be consistent with the regulations prescribed by the Secretary of Labor to carry out the FMLA's Title I. 5 U.S.C.A. § 6387.

E. TITLE III—COMMISSION ON FMLA LEAVE

1. TITLE III—GENERALLY

Title III established a bipartisan commission to investigate and prepare a report regarding:

1. The FMLA's impact on employers and employees;

2. A review of state family and medical leave laws; and

3. Investigate potential additional legislation to provide leave benefits for employees not covered by the FMLA. 29 U.S.C.A. §§ 2631–2636.

2. DUTIES

The Commission's duties were to conduct a comprehensive survey of:

1. Existing and proposed mandatory and voluntary policies relating to family and temporary medical leaves, including policies provided by employers not covered by the FMLA;

2. The potential costs, benefits, and impact on productivity, job creation, and business growth of these policies on employees and employers;

3. Possible differences in costs, benefits, and the impact on productivity, job creation, and business growth of these policies on employers based on business type and size;

4. The impact of FMLA policies on the availability of employee benefits provided by employers, including employers not covered by the FMLA;

5. Alternate and equivalent state enforcement of the FMLA's Title I with respect to employees;

6. Methods used by employers to reduce administrative costs of implementing FMLA policies;

7. The ability of employers to recover lost health care premiums when employees fail to return to work; and

8. The impact on employees and employers of FMLA policies that provide temporary wage replacement during periods of FMLA leave. 29 U.S.C.A. § 2632.

Two years from the date that the FMLA Commission first met it was required to prepare and submit to the appropriate Committees of Congress a report concerning these matters. The Commission, chaired by Senator Christopher Dodd (D–Conn.), was formed in 1993 and disbanded in 1996 following completion of its investigation and issuance of its report. See Chapter 1 for a discussion of the Commission's Report: REPORT OF THE COMMISSION ON FAMILY AND MEDICAL LEAVE, A WORKABLE BALANCE: REPORT TO THE CONGRESS ON FAMILY AND MEDICAL LEAVE POLICIES (April 30, 1996).

F. TITLE IV—MISCELLANEOUS PROVISIONS

1. TITLE IV—GENERALLY

Title IV includes provisions for integrating the FMLA with state laws, a statement of non-discrimination, and establishment of regulations to be provided by the Department of Labor (DOL) within 120 days of the FMLA's signing. 29 U.S.C.A. §§ 2651–2654.

2. EFFECT ON OTHER LAWS

a. Federal and State Antidiscrimination Laws

Nothing in the FMLA or in any amendment to the FMLA modifies or affects any federal or state law prohibiting discrimination on the basis of race, religion, color, national origin, sex, age, or disability. 29 U.S.C.A. § 2651(a).

b. State and Local Laws

Nothing in the FMLA or in any amendment to the FMLA supersedes any provision of any state or local law that provides greater family or medical leave rights than the rights established under the FMLA or in any amendment to the FMLA. 29 U.S.C.A. § 2651(b).

3. EFFECT ON EXISTING EMPLOYMENT BENEFITS

a. More Protective

Nothing in the FMLA or in any amendment to the FMLA diminishes the obligation of an employer to comply with any collective bargaining agreement or any employment benefit program or plan that provides greater family or medical leave rights to employees than the rights established by the FMLA or any amendment to the FMLA. 29 U.S.C.A. § 2652(a).

b. Less Protective

The rights established for employees under the FMLA or any amendment to the FMLA cannot be diminished by any collective bargaining agreement or any employment benefit program or plan. 29 U.S.C.A. § 2652(b).

4. ENCOURAGEMENT OF MORE GENEROUS FMLA LEAVE

Nothing in the FMLA or in any amendment to the FMLA prevents employers from adopting or retaining leave policies that are more generous than any policies complying with the FMLA's requirements or any amendment to the FMLA. 29 U.S.C.A. § 2653.

5.   REGULATIONS

The Secretary of Labor was given the authority to prescribe any regulations to implement the FMLA's Title I and Title IV not later than one hundred-twenty days after the date of the FMLA's enactment. 29 U.S.C.A. § 2654.

6.   EFFECTIVE DATES

The effective dates for the FMLA are as follows:

1.   Title III took effect on the date of the FMLA's enactment and

2.   Titles I, II, and V took effect six months after the date of the FMLA's enactment except for collective bargaining agreements in effect on the FMLA's effective date for which the FMLA was not effective until the earlier of:

    a.   The date of the collective bargaining agreement's termination or

    b.   The date that occurred twelve months after the date of the FMLA's enactment. 29 U.S.C.A. § 2601 note.

G. TITLE V—COVERAGE OF CONGRESSIONAL EMPLOYEES

1. TITLE V—GENERALLY

Title V provides FMLA coverage for employees of the United States House of Representatives and Senate. The original Title V, however, was subsequently repealed in 1995. Its sections were recodified by the Congressional Accountability Act of 1995. 2 U.S.C.A. §§ 60m, 60n, *repealed by*, 2 U.S.C.A. §§ 1301, 1302, 1312, 1381–1385, 1401–1416.

The Congressional Accountability Act of 1995 was adopted to make certain employment standards and discrimination legislation applicable to the United States House of Representatives and Senate. It made the following statutes applicable to the legislative branch of the federal government:

1. Fair Labor Standards Act (FLSA) [29 U.S.C.A. §§ 201–219];

2. Civil Rights Act of 1964 (Title VII) [42 U.S.C.A. §§ 2000e–1 to 2002–17];

3. Americans with Disabilities Act (ADA) [42 U.S.C.A. §§ 12101–12213];

4. Age Discrimination in Employment Act (ADEA) [29 U.S.C.A. §§ 621–634];

5. Family and Medical Leave Act (FMLA) [2 U.S.C.A. §§ 1301, 1302, 1312, 1381–1385,

1401–1416; 5 U.S.C.A. §§ 6381–6387; 29 U.S.C.A. §§ 2601–2654];

6. Occupational Safety and Health Act (OSHA) [29 U.S.C.A. §§ 651–678];

7. Chapter 71 relating to Federal Service Labor–Management Relations [5 U.S.C.A. §§ 7101 et seq.];

8. Employee Polygraph Protection Act (EPPA) [29 U.S.C.A. §§ 2001–2009];

9. Worker Adjustment and Retraining Notification Act (WARN) [29 U.S.C.A. §§ 2101–2108];

10. Rehabilitation Act of 1973 [29 U.S.C.A. §§ 701–794]; and

11. Veterans' Employment and Reemployment [38 U.S.C.A. §§ 2021(a)(A), 2021(a)(B), 2021(b)(1), 2024]. 2 U.S.C.A. § 1302.

The Congressional Accountability Act of 1995, specifically provided that the FMLA's rights and protections under Title I were applicable to employees of the Senate and the House of Representatives. 2 U.S.C.A. § 1302, 1312, 1381–1385, 1401–1416.

2. COMPLAINTS

Under the Congressional Accountability Act of 1995, the Office of Compliance was given the authority to review FMLA complaints and an administrative and judicial dispute-resolution procedure was created. 2 U.S.C.A. §§ 1381–1385, 1401–1416. Employees were given the right to:

1. Request counseling by filing a complaint;

2. Request mediation;

3. A hearing before a hearing officer;

4. Appeal to the Office of Compliance's Board of Directors;

5. File for judicial review of the Office of Compliance's Board of Directors' decisions; and

6. Commence a civil action before a district court of the United States after completion of counseling and mediation. 2 U.S.C.A. §§ 1402–1408.

3. REMEDIES

The Congressional Accountability Act of 1995 makes certain of the FMLA's remedies under Title I applicable to employees of the Senate and the House of Representatives. 2 U.S.C.A. § 1312(b). Violation of the FMLA can result in the following remedies being assessed:

1. *General Damages.* Damages equal to the amount of any wages, salary, employment benefits, or other compensation denied or lost to the employee by reason of violating the FMLA plus:

    a. Interest. The interest on this amount calculated at the prevailing rate and

    b. Liquidated Damages. An additional amount as liquidated damages equal to the sum of the amount permitted as damages and interest unless the employer can prove to the court's satisfaction that the act or omission that caused the FMLA violation was in good faith and that the employer had reasonable grounds for believing that the act or omission was not an FMLA violation and the court may,in its discretion, reduce the liability for the liquidated damages amount to the amount permitted as damages and interest.

2. *Actual Monetary Loss.* In a case where wages, salary, employment benefits, or other compensation have not been denied or lost to the employee, any actual monetary losses sustained by the employee as a direct result of the violation, for example, the cost of providing care, up to a sum equal to twelve weeks of wages for the employee.

3. *Equitable Relief.* Any equitable relief that the court may find appropriate. 2 U.S.C.A. § 1312(b); 29 U.S.C.A. § 2617(a)(1).

4. *Attorney's Fees, Expert Witness Fees, Costs, etc.* The court in any action where the plaintiff is awarded a judgment must allow reasonable attorney's fees, reasonable expert witness fees, and other costs of the action to be paid by the defendant. 2 U.S.C.A. § 1312(b); 29 U.S.C.A. §§ 2617(a)(3).

H. TITLE VI—SENSE OF CONGRESS

1. TITLE VI—GENERALLY

Title VI is a rider that required the Secretary of the Department of Defense to review its policies with respect to the service of homosexuals in the armed forces. Pub. L. No. 103–3, 107 Stat. 6, § 601 (Feb. 5, 1993).

2. SENSE OF CONGRESS REGARDING HOMOSEXUALS IN THE ARMED SERVICES

Regarding homosexuals in the Armed Services, it was the sense of Congress that:

1. The Secretary of Defense conduct a comprehensive review of current departmental policy with respect to the service of homosexuals in the Armed Forces;

2. This review was to include the:

    a. Basis for the current policy of mandatory separation;

    b. Rights of all service men and women; and

    c. Effects of any change in this policy on morale, discipline, and military effectiveness.

3. The Secretary was required to report the results of this review and consultation and recommendations to the President of the United States and to the Congress no later than July 15, 1993; and

4. The Senate Committee on Armed Services was required to conduct:

a. Comprehensive hearings on the current military policy with respect to the service of homosexuals in the military services and

b. Oversight hearings on the Secretary's recommendations as these were reported. Pub. L. No. 103–3, 107 Stat. 6, § 601 (Feb. 5, 1993).

CHAPTER 3

STATE FAMILY AND MEDICAL LEAVE REGULATION

A. INTRODUCTION

Over thirty states require employers to provide some form of family and/or medical leave. The federal Family and Medical Leave Act (FMLA) of 1993 does not preempt a state statute from providing more generous leave rights and benefits. 29 U.S.C.A. § 2651(b); 29 C.F.R. § 825.701. In most instances, however, the FMLA is more generous to employees and must be followed. Where the employer is not covered by the FMLA, the employer may still be subject to a state family and/or medical leave statute.

The key to understanding these state family and medical leave statutes lies in recognizing any interplay between the state statute and the FMLA. This chapter identifies these state statutes and their potential effect upon the FMLA.

B. OVERVIEW OF STATE LEGISLATION

The following states offer some form of family and/or medical leave for either private or public sector employees or both:

1. *Alabama:* Family leave. Ala. Admin. Code §§ 670–X–14–.01, 670–X–14–.02.

2. *Alaska:* Family leave. Alaska Stat. §§ 14.20.140, 14.20.145, 14.20.590, 23.10.500, 23.10.510, 23.10.520, 23.10.530, 23.10.540, 23.10.550, 23.40.200, 39.20.225, 39.20.305, 42.40.860.

3. *Arizona:* Parental leave. Ariz. Admin. Comp. R. 2–5–104, 2–5–207, 2–5–404, 2–5–411, 2–5–702.

4. *California:* Family and medical leave. Cal. Gov't Code §§ 12945.1, 12945.2.

5. *Colorado:* Family leave. Colo. C.R. P7–2–5, P7–7–1 to P7–7–4.

6. *Connecticut:* Family and medical leave. Conn. Gen. Stat. §§ 31–51cc to 31–51gg.

7. *Delaware:* Adoption leave. Del. Code Ann. tit. 29, § 5116.

8. *District of Columbia:* Family and medical leave. D.C. Code Ann. §§ 36–1301 to 36–1317.

9. *Florida:* Family leave. Fla. Stat. Ann. § 110.221.

10. *Georgia:* Family leave. Ga. Code Ann. §§ 23.100—23.803.

11. *Hawaii:* Family and medical leave. Haw. Code Ann. §§ 398–1 to 398–10.

12. *Idaho:* Family and medical leave. Idaho Code §§ 28.01.01240 to 28.01.01244.

13. *Illinois:* Adoption and child care leave. Ill. Admin. Code § 420.645.

14. *Iowa:* Family leave. Iowa Admin. Code §§ 581–1, 581–14.3(11), 581–14.4.

15. *Kansas:* Family leave. Kan. Admin. R. 1–9–5 to 1–9–27.

16. *Kentucky:* Family leave. Ky. Rev. Stat. Ann. § 161.155(a).

17. *Maine:* Family and medical leave. Me. Rev. Stat. Ann. tit. 26, §§ 843–849.

18. *Maryland:* Family leave. Md. State. Pers. Code Ann. §§ 9–1001, 9–501 to 9–508.

19. *Missouri:* Family and medical leave. Mo. Rev. Stat. §§ 20–5.020.

20. *Montana:* Parental leave. Mont. Rev. Code § 2–18–606.

21. *Nebraska:* Family leave. Neb. Admin. Code ch. 9. § 005.01D.

22. *Nevada:* Adoption and infant care leave. Nev. Rev. Stat. § 284.360.

23. *New Jersey:* Family and medical leave. N.J. Rev. Stat. §§ 34:11B–1 to 34:11B–16.

24. *North Carolina:* Family leave. N.C. Admin. Code tit. 25, § .0305.

25. *North Dakota:* Family leave. N.D. Cent. Code §§ 54–52.4–01 to 54–52.4–10.

26. *Oklahoma:* Family leave. Okla. Stat. tit. 74, § 840.7c.

27. *Oregon:* Family and medical leave. Or. Rev. Stat. §§ 659.470 to 659.494.

28. *Rhode Island:* Family and medical leave. R.I. Gen. Laws §§ 28–48–1 to 28–48–11.

29. *South Carolina:* Family leave. S.C. Code §§ 8–11–40, 8–11–155.

30. *South Dakota:* Family leave. Admin. Rules S.D. § 55:01:22:02:04.

31. *Utah:* Family and medical leave. Utah Admin. Code §§ 477–8–7.(4), 477–8–7.(10), 477–8–9 to 477–8–13.

32. *Vermont:* Family and medical leave. Vt. Stat. Ann. tit. 21, §§ 470–474.

33. *Washington:* Adoption and child care leave. Wash. Rev. Code §§ 49.12.005, 49.12.270, 49.12.275, 49.12.280, 49.12.285, 49.12.290, 49.12.295, 49.12.350, 49.12.360, 49.12.370, 49–78.010 to 49.78.901.

34. *West Virginia:* Family leave. W. Va. Code Ann. §§ 21–5D–1 to 21–5D–9.

35. *Wisconsin:* Family and medical leave. Wis. Stat. Ann. §§ 103.10, 893.96, 230.35.

The most comprehensive state statutes applicable to the private and the public sector require employers to grant employees of either sex unpaid leaves for the birth or adoption of a child or for the serious illness of an immediate family member. For example, the following statutes illustrate these types of family leave laws:

1. California. Cal. Gov't Code §§ 12945.1, 12945.2.

2. Connecticut. Conn. Gen. Stat. §§ 31–51cc to 31–51gg.

3. District of Columbia. D.C. Code Ann. §§ 36–1301 to 36–1317.

4. Hawaii. Haw. Code Ann. §§ 398–1 to 398–10.

5. Maine. Me. Rev. Stat. Ann. tit. 26, §§ 843—849.

6. New Jersey. N.J. Rev. Stat. §§ 34:11B–1 to 34:11B–16.

7. Oregon. Or. Rev. Stat. §§ 659.470 to 659.494.

8. Rhode Island. R.I. Gen. Laws §§ 28–48–1 to 28–48–11.

9. Vermont. Vt. Stat. Ann. tit. 21, §§ 470–474.

10. Wisconsin. Wis. Stat. Ann. §§ 103.10, 893.96, 230.35.

To be eligible for leave, these statutes require that employees must work for the employer for a specified time period, for example:

1. *California:* One year of continuous service. Cal. Gov't Code §§ 12945.1, 12945.2.

2. *Connecticut:* Twelve months and 1000 hours of service. Conn. Gen. Stat. §§ 31–51cc to 31–51gg.

3. *District of Columbia:* Twelve months and 1000 hours of service. D.C. Code Ann. §§ 36–1301 to 36–1317.

4. *Hawaii:* Six months. Haw. Code Ann. §§ 398–1 to 398–10.

5. *Maine:* Twelve consecutive months. Me. Rev. Stat. Ann. tit. 26, §§ 843–849.

6. *New Jersey:* Twelve months and 1000 hours of service. N.J. Rev. Stat. §§ 34:11B–1 to 34:11B–16.

7. *Oregon:* 180 days. Or. Rev. Stat. §§ 659.470 to 659.494.

8. *Rhode Island:* Twelve months. R.I. Gen. Laws §§ 28–48–1 to 28–48–11.

9. *Vermont:* One year for an average of 30 hours per week. Vt. Stat. Ann. tit. 21, §§ 470–474.

10. *Wisconsin:* 52 weeks and 1000 hours. Wis. Stat. Ann. §§ 103.10, 893.96, 230.35.

The required leave's length varies from four weeks in one calendar year to four months in a twenty-four month period, for example:

1. *California:* Four months in a twenty-four month period. Cal. Gov't Code §§ 12945.1, 12945.2.

2. Connecticut: Sixteen weeks in a two year period. Conn. Gen. Stat. §§ 31–51cc to 31–51gg.

3. *District of Columbia:* Sixteen weeks in a twenty-four month period. D.C. Code Ann. §§ 36–1301 to 36–1317.

4. *Hawaii:* Four weeks in a calendar year. Haw. Code Ann. §§ 398–1 to 398–10.

5. *Maine:* Ten weeks in two years. Me. Rev. Stat. Ann. tit. 26, §§ 843–849.

6. *New Jersey:* Twelve weeks in a twenty-four month period. N.J. Rev. Stat. §§ 34:11B–1 to 34:11B–16.

7. *Oregon:* Twelve weeks in two years. Or. Rev. Stat. §§ 659.470 to 659.494.

8. *Rhode Island:* Thirteen weeks in two years. R.I. Gen. Laws §§ 28–48–1 to 28–48–11.

9. *Vermont:* Twelve weeks in twelve months. Vt. Stat. Ann. tit. 21, §§ 470–474.

10. *Wisconsin:* Two to eight weeks in twelve months depending on the reasons. Wis. Stat. Ann. §§ 103.10, 893.96, 230.35.

Employees are generally required to give advance notice for a leave whenever possible. Medical certification of the illness may also be required by the employer, for example:

1. California. Cal. Gov't Code §§ 12945.1, 12945.2.

2. District of Columbia. D.C. Code Ann. §§ 36–1301 to 36–1317.

3. Hawaii. Haw. Code Ann. §§ 398–1 to 398–10.

4. Maine. Me. Rev. Stat. Ann. tit. 26, §§ 843–849.

5. New Jersey. N.J. Rev. Stat. §§ 34:11B–1 to 34:11B–16.

6. Wisconsin. Wis. Stat. Ann. §§ 103.10, 893.96, 230.35.

In some states, employers may deny family leave to certain highly compensated employees. The employer, however, generally must demonstrate its need to deny the leave and give the employee notice of the decision, for example:

1. *California:* Undue hardship, or if the employee is among the five highest paid employees or in the top ten percent (10%). Cal. Gov't Code §§ 12945.1, 12945.2.

2. *District of Columbia:* Five highest paid employees or among the highest paid ten percent (10%), depending on the employer's size. D.C. Code Ann. §§ 36–1301 to 36–1317.

3. *New Jersey:* Highest paid five percent (5%) or among the seven highest paid employees. N.J. Rev. Stat. §§ 34:11B–1 to 34:11B–16.

C. FMLA PREEMPTION OF STATE REGULATION

The FMLA does not preempt state and local statutes or laws providing more generous leave rights. 29 U.S.C.A. § 2651(b); 29 C.F.R. § 825.701. For example, a state's leave statute may apply to smaller employers that are not covered by the

FMLA. The FMLA permits these state laws to continue to operate. Eligible employees may take leave under the state law, even though they have no rights under the FMLA.

When the requisite coverage or applicability standards of both statutes are met and the statutes contain differing provisions, an analysis must be made of both statutes, provision-by-provision, to determine which standard(s) from each statute will apply to the particular situation. 29 C.F.R. § 825.701. The standard providing the greater right or more generous benefit to the employee from each statutory provision-by-provision will apply. However, leave taken for a reason specified in both the federal and state statutes may be simultaneously counted against the employee's entitlement under both statutes. 29 C.F.R. § 825.701.

For example, if a state workers' compensation statute provides a job guarantee to employees who are temporarily out of work due to occupational injuries and it is more generous than the FMLA's job restoration provisions, this statute is a "State ... law that provides greater ... medical leave rights ..." [29 U.S.C.A. § 2651(b)] and would govern the employee's reinstatement. 29 C.F.R. § 825.701.

A more difficult problem occurs when an employer is covered by both the FMLA and a state leave statute. The Department of Labor (DOL) in the FMLA's regulations has taken the position that if leave qualifies under both the FMLA and the state statute, the leave used counts against the employee's entitlement under both statutes. 29 C.F.R. § 825.701. For example, if the state statute provides for sixteen weeks of leave in a two year period, the employee would be entitled to take sixteen weeks one year under the state statute and twelve weeks the next under the FMLA.

CHAPTER 4

BENEFIT AND LEAVE GUIDE- LINES UNDER THE FAMILY AND MEDICAL LEAVE ACT'S (FMLA'S) REGULATIONS

A. INTRODUCTION

The Family and Medical Leave Act (FMLA) of 1993 required the Department of Labor (DOL) to issue regulations to implement the FMLA's Titles I and IV. 29 U.S.C.A. § 2654; 29 C.F.R. §§ 825.100–825.800. Instead of giving employers a wide range of latitude in the FMLA's administration within their organizations, the DOL's regulations are highly detailed procedures on leave eligibility, notification, approval, and return to work. 29 C.F.R. §§ 825.100–825.800.

These details make the FMLA's regulations important for employees and employers. They set forth the manner in which the FMLA's rights and benefits are exercised. This chapter reviews the FMLA's statutory and regulatory provisions relating to:

1. Leave reasons;

2. Leave eligibility;

3. Leave amount;

4. Paid or unpaid leave;

5. Intermittent or reduced leave schedule;

6. Benefit continuation;

7. More generous benefits;

8. Outside employment while on leave;

9. Medical certification;

10. Fraudulent FMLA leave; and

11. Restoration to position rights.

B. LEAVE REASONS

Employers covered by the FMLA are required to grant leave to eligible employees:

1. For the birth of a daughter or son, and to care for the newborn child;

2. For the placement with the employee of a daughter or son for adoption or foster care;

3. To care for the employee's spouse, daughter, son, or parent with a serious health condition; and

4. For a serious health condition that makes the employee unable to perform the functions of the employee's job. 29 U.S.C.A. § 2612(a); 29 C.F.R. § 825.112.

1. RIGHT OF FEMALES AND MALES TO LEAVE

The right to take an FMLA leave applies equally to female and male employees. 29 C.F.R.

§ 825.112(b). A mother and father can take family leave for a child's birth, placement for adoption, or foster care.

2. EFFECT OF LAYOFF AND OTHER EMPLOYMENT INTERRUPTIONS

In situations where the employment relationship has been interrupted (for example, a layoff), the employee must be recalled or otherwise be re-employed before being eligible for FMLA leave. 29 C.F.R. § 825.112(f).

3. BIRTH OF A CHILD

Circumstances may require that FMLA leave begin before the child's birth. 29 C.F.R. § 825.112(c). For example, an expectant mother may take FMLA leave before the child's birth for prenatal care or if her condition makes her unable to work.

4. PLACEMENT FOR ADOPTION OR FOSTER CARE

Employers are required to grant FMLA leave before a child's actual placement or adoption if a work absence is required for the adoption placement or foster care to proceed. 29 C.F.R. § 825.112(d). This may require the employee to:

1. Attend counselling sessions;

2. Appear in court;

3. Consult with his or her attorney or the doctor(s) representing the birth parent; or

4. Undergo a physical examination.

The source of an adopted child whether from a licensed placement agency or otherwise is not a factor in determining this leave's eligibility.

Foster care is twenty-four hour care for children in substitution for, and away from, their:

1. Parents or

2. Guardian. 29 C.F.R. § 825.112(e).

It involves an agreement between the state and foster family that the foster family will take care of the child. Although foster care may be with the child's relatives, state action is involved in the removal of the child from parental custody. This placement is made by or with the state's agreement:

1. As a result of a voluntary agreement between the parent or guardian that the child be removed from the home or

2. Pursuant to a judicial determination for the foster care's necessity. 29 C.F.R. § 825.112(e).

5. SERIOUS HEALTH CONDITION

A "serious health condition" means an illness, injury, impairment, or physical or mental condition that involves:

1. Inpatient Care; that is an overnight stay in a hospital, hospice, or residential medical care facility, including any period of incapacity (an inability to work, attend school or perform

other regular daily activities due to the serious health condition, treatment therefor, or recovery therefrom), or any subsequent treatment in connection with this inpatient care; or

2. Continuing treatment by a health care provider; that is any one or more of the following:

    a. A period of incapacity, that is an inability to work, attend school or perform other regular daily activities due to the serious health condition treatment therefor, or recovery therefrom of more than three consecutive calendar days, and any subsequent treatment or period of incapacity relating to the same condition, that also involves:

        i. Treatment two or more times by a health care provider, by a nurse or physician's assistant under direct supervision of a health care provider, or by a provider of health care services (for example, a physical therapist) under orders of, or on referral by, a health care provider or

        ii. Treatment by a health care provider on at least one occasion which results in a regimen of continuing treatment under the supervision of the health care provider.

    b. Any period of incapacity due to pregnancy, or for prenatal care.

c. Any period of incapacity or treatment for this incapacity or treatment due to a chronic serious health condition. A chronic serious health condition is one which:

    i. Requires periodic visits for treatment by a health care provider, or by a nurse or physician's assistant under direct supervision of a health care provider;

    ii. Continues over an extended period of time, including recurring episodes of a single underlying condition; and

    iii. May cause episodic rather than a continuing period of incapacity (for example, asthma, diabetes, epilepsy, etc.).

d. A period of incapacity which is permanent or long-term due to a condition for which treatment may not be effective. The employee or family member must be under the continuing supervision of, but need not be receiving active treatment by, a health care provider. Examples include Alzheimer's, a severe stroke, or the terminal stages of a disease.

e. Any period of absence to receive multiple treatments, including any period of recovery therefrom, by a health care provider or by a provider of health care services under orders of, or on referral by, a health care provider, either for restorative surgery after an accident or other injury, or for a condition that would likely result in a period of incapacity of more than three consecutive calendar days in the absence of medical intervention or treatment, such as cancer (for example, chemotherapy, radiation, etc.) severe arthritis (physical therapy), kidney disease (dialysis). 29 U.S.C.A. § 2611(11); 29 C.F.R. § 825.114.

A regimen of continuing treatment includes, for example:

1. A course of prescription medication (for example, an antibiotic) or

2. Therapy requiring special equipment to resolve or alleviate the health condition or alleviate the health condition (for example, oxygen).

A regimen of continuing treatment that includes the taking of over-the-counter medications such as aspirin, antihistamines, or salves; or bedrest, drinking fluids, exercise and other similar activities that can be initiated without a visit to a health care provider, is not, by itself, sufficient to constitute a regimen of continuing treatment for an FMLA leave.

Treatment includes, but is not limited to:

1. Examinations to determine if a serious health condition exists and

2. Evaluations of the condition.

Treatment does not include:

1. Routine physical examinations;

2. Eye examinations; or

3. Dental examinations.

Conditions for which cosmetic treatments are administered (for example, most treatments for acne or plastic surgery) are not "serious health conditions" unless inpatient hospital care is required or unless complications develop.

Ordinarily, unless complications arise, the following are examples of conditions that do not meet the definition of a serious health condition and do not qualify for FMLA leave:

1. The common cold;

2. The flu;

3. Ear aches;

4. Upset stomach;

5. Minor ulcers;

6. Headaches other than migraine;

7. Routine dental or orthodontia problems; and

8. Periodontal disease.

Restorative dental or plastic surgery after an injury or removal of cancerous growths are serious health conditions provided all the other conditions for a serious health condition are met.

Mental illness resulting from stress or allergies may be serious health conditions, but only if all the conditions for a serious health condition are met.

Substance abuse may be a serious health condition. FMLA leave may only be taken for treatment for substance abuse through a:

1. Health care provider or

2. Provider of health care services on referral by a health care provider.

Absence because of the employee's use of the substance, rather than for treatment, does not qualify for FMLA leave.

Absences attributable to incapacity qualify for FMLA leave even though the employee or the immediate family member does not receive treatment from a health care provider during the absence, and even if the absence does not last more than three days. For example, an employee with asthma may be unable to report for work due to the onset of an asthma attack or because the employee's health care provider has advised the employee to stay home when the pollen count exceeds a certain level. An employee who is pregnant may be unable to report to work because of severe morning sickness.

6.   SUBSTANCE ABUSE TREATMENT

FMLA leave is available for substance abuse treatment. 29 C.F.R. §§ 825.112(g), 825.114. However, substance abuse treatment does not prevent an employer from taking an adverse employment action against an employee. If the employer has an established policy, applied in a non-discriminatory manner that has been communicated to all employees, that an employee may be terminated for substance abuse, the employee may be terminated whether or not the employee is taking FMLA leave.

An employee may take FMLA leave to care for an immediate family member who is receiving substance abuse treatment. 29 C.F.R. §§ 825.112(g), 825.114. The employer may not take action against an employee who is providing care for an immediate family member receiving substance abuse treatment.

7. FAMILY MEMBER CARE

The medical certification provision that an employee is "needed to care for" a family member encompasses both:

1. Physical and

2. Psychological care. 29 C.F.R. § 825.116(a).

It includes situations where because of a serious health condition, the family member is unable to:

1. Care for his or her own basic medical, hygienic, or nutritional needs or safety or

2. Transport himself or herself to the doctor, etc. 29 C.F.R. § 825.116(a).

It also includes providing psychological comfort and reassurance which would be beneficial to a spouse, child, or parent with a serious health condition who is receiving inpatient or home care. 29 C.F.R. § 825.116(a). The term also encompasses situations where the employee may be needed to:

1. Fill in for others who are caring for the family member or

2. Make arrangements for changes in care, such as transfer to a nursing home. 29 C.F.R. § 825.116(b).

An employee's intermittent leave or a reduced leave schedule necessary to care for a family member includes:

1. Where the family member's condition itself is intermittent and the employee is only needed intermittently where other care is normally available or

2. Care responsibilities are shared with another member of the family or a third party. 29 C.F.R. § 825.116(c).

C. LEAVE ELIGIBILITY

An "eligible employee" for FMLA leave is an employee of a covered employer who:

1. Has been employed by the employer for at least twelve months; and

2. Has been employed for at least 1,250 hours of service during the twelve month period immediately preceding the commencement of the leave; and

3. Is employed at a worksite where fifty or more employees are employed by the employer within seventy-five miles of that worksite. 29 U.S.C.A. § 2611(2); 29 C.F.R. § 825.110.

1. MONTH REQUIREMENT

a. **Full-time and Part-time Employees**

The twelve months an employee must have been employed by the employer need not be consecutive months. 29 C.F.R. § 825.110(b). If an employee is maintained on the payroll for any part of a week, including any periods of paid or unpaid leave (for example, sick or vacation) during which the employee provides other benefits or compensation (for example, workers' compensation, group health plan benefits, etc.), the week counts as a week of employment regardless of whether the employee is full-time or part-time.

b. **Intermittent, Occasional, and Casual Employees**

For purposes of determining whether intermittent, occasional, or casual employment qualifies as "at least twelve months," fifty-two weeks is deemed to be equal to twelve months. 29 C.F.R. § 825.110(b).

2. HOUR REQUIREMENT

Whether an employee has worked the minimum 1,250 hours of service is determined according to the Fair Labor Standards Act (FLSA). 29 C.F.R. § 825.110(c); see also 29 C.F.R. Part 785. The determining factor is the number of hours an employee has worked for the employer within the FLSA's meaning.

The determination is not limited by recordkeeping methods, or by compensation agreements that do not accurately reflect all of the hours an employee has worked for or been in the employer's service. Any accurate accounting of actual hours worked under the FLSA's principles may be used.

If an employer does not maintain an accurate record of hours worked by an employee, including for employees who are exempt from the FLSA's requirement that a record be kept of their hours worked (for example, bona fide executive, administrative, and professional employees as defined in the FLSA's Regulations [see 29 C.F.R. Part 541]), the employer has the burden of showing that the employee has not worked the requisite hours. 29 C.F.R. § 825.110(c). Should the employer be unable to meet this burden, the employee is deemed to have met the eligibility test.

Full-time teachers of an elementary or secondary school system, or institution of higher education, or other educational establishment or institution are deemed to meet the 1,250 hour test. 29 C.F.R. § 825.110(c). The employer must be able to clearly demonstrate that this employee did not work 1,250 hours during the previous twelve months to claim that the employee is not "eligible" for FMLA leave.

The determinations of whether an employee has worked for the employer for at least 1,250 hours in the past twelve months and has been employed by the employer for a total of at least twelve months must be made as of the date leave commences. 29

C.F.R. § 825.110(d). If an employee notifies the employer of a need for FMLA leave before the employee meets these eligibility criteria, the employer must either:

1. Confirm the employee's eligibility based upon a projection that the employee will be eligible on the date leave would commence or

2. Advise the employee when the eligibility requirement will be met. 29 C.F.R. § 825.110(d).

Should the employer confirm eligibility at the time the leave's notice is received, the employer may not subsequently challenge the employee's eligibility. If the employer does not advise the employee whether the employee is eligible as soon as practicable (for example, two business days absent extenuating circumstances) after the date that employee eligibility is determined, the employee will have satisfied the notice requirements and the leave notice is considered current and outstanding until the employer does advise. 29 C.F.R. § 825.110(d).

If the employer fails to advise the employee whether the employee is eligible prior to the date the requested FMLA leave commences, the employee will be deemed eligible. 29 C.F.R. § 825.110(d). The employer may not, then, deny the leave.

Where the employee does not give notice of the need for leave more than two business days prior to commencing leave, the employee will be deemed to be eligible if the employer fails to advise the employee that the employee is not eligible within two business days of receiving the employee's notice. 29 C.F.R. § 825.110(d).

> NOTE: The above FMLA regulations have been challenged and in certain federal court circuits may be invalid. See *Seaman v. Downtown Partnership*, 991 F.Supp. 751 (D.Md.1998) (this regulation contradicts Congress' intent regarding employee eligibility; i.e, if the employee is ineligible for FMLA leave, the employer cannot on its own action confer statutory FMLA status on the employee); *Wolke v. Dreadnought Marine, Inc.*, 954 F.Supp. 1133 (E.D.Va.1997) (the Department of Labor (DOL) usurped the legislature's and judiciary's constitutional authority in making an employee eligible for FMLA leave unless the employee is given notice of ineligibility from the employer within two days after it receives the employee's leave request); see also *Cox v. Autozone, Inc.*, 990 F.Supp. 1369 (M.D.Ala.1998) (the FMLA's regulations convert an employer's statutory right to require an employee to substitute employer-provided paid leave for unpaid FMLA leave into an employee entitlement to more than twelve weeks of leave).

3. WORKSITE

a. When Determined

Whether fifty employees are employed within seventy-five miles to ascertain an employee's FMLA eligibility is determined when the employee gives notice of the need for leave. 29 C.F.R. § 825.110(f).

Once an employee is determined eligible in response to that notice of the leave's need, the employee's eligibility is not affected by any subsequent change in the number of employees employed at or within seventy-five miles of the employee's worksite for that leave.

b. Worksite Number Change after Leave Commences

The employer may not terminate an employee's FMLA leave that has already commenced if the employee-count drops below fifty at the worksite. 29 C.F.R. § 825.110(f). For example, if an employer employs sixty employees in August, but expects that the number of employees will drop to forty in December, the employer must grant FMLA leave to an otherwise eligible employee who gives notice of the need for leave in August for a period of leave to begin in December.

c. Worksite Description

Generally, a worksite can refer to either a:

1. Single location or
2. Group of contiguous locations. 29 C.F.R. § 825.111(a).

Structures which form a campus or industrial park, or separate facilities in proximity with one another, may be considered a single employment site. 29 C.F.R. § 825.111(a).

There may be several single employment sites within a single building, such as an office building, if separate employers conduct activities within the building. 29 C.F.R. § 825.111(a). For example, an office building with fifty different businesses as tenants will contain fifty employment sites. The offices of each employer will be considered separate employment sites for the FMLA's purposes.

An employee's FMLA worksite is ordinarily the site the employee reports to or, if none, from which the employee's work is assigned. 29 C.F.R. § 825.111(a). Separate buildings or areas not directly connected or in immediate proximity are a single worksite if they:

1. Are in reasonable geographic proximity;

2. Are used for the same purpose; and

3. Share the same staff and equipment. 29 C.F.R. § 825.111(a)(1).

For example, if an employer manages a number of warehouses in a metropolitan area but regularly shifts or rotates the same employees from one building to another, the multiple warehouses would be a single worksite.

d. No–Fixed Worksite—Generally

For employees with no fixed worksite, the "worksite" is the site to which they are assigned as their home base, from which their work is assigned, or to which they report. 29 C.F.R. § 825.111(a)(2). This includes construction workers, transportation workers, truck drivers, seamen, pilots, salespersons, etc.

e. No–Fixed Worksite—Construction Workers

For construction workers, the worksite is the site:

1. To which they are assigned as their home base;

2. From which their work is assigned; or

3. To which they report. 29 C.F.R. § 825.111(a)(2).

For example, if a construction company headquartered in New Jersey opened a construction site in Ohio, and set up a mobile trailer on the construction site as the company's on-site office, the construction site in Ohio would be the worksite for any employees hired locally who report to the mobile trailer/company office daily for work assignments, etc. If that construction company also sent personnel such as job superintendents, foremen, engineers, an office manager, etc., from New Jersey to the job site in Ohio, those workers sent from New Jersey continue to have the headquarters in New Jersey as their "worksite." The workers who have New Jersey as their worksite would not be counted in determining the eligibility of employees whose home base is the Ohio worksite, but would be counted in determining eligibility of employees whose home base is New Jersey.

f. No–Fixed Worksite—Transportation Employees

For transportation employees, their worksite is the terminal to which they:

1. Are assigned;

2. Report for work;

3. Depart; and

4. Return after completion of a work assignment. 29 C.F.R. § 825.111(a)(2).

For example, an airline pilot may work for an airline with headquarters in New York, but the pilot regularly reports for duty and originates or begins flights from the company's facilities located at a Chicago airport and returns to Chicago at the completion of one or more flights to go off duty. The pilot's worksite is the Chicago facility.

g. No–Fixed Worksite—Employee's Personal Residence

An employee's personal residence is not a worksite in the case of:

1. Salespersons who travel a sales territory and who generally leave to work and return from work to their personal residence or

2. Employees who work at home under a flexiplace concept. 29 C.F.R. § 825.111(a)(2).

These employees' worksite is the office to which they report and from which assignments are made.

h. Joint Employment Worksite

For purposes of determining an employee's eligibility, when an employee is jointly employed by two or more employers, the employee's worksite is the primary employer's office from which the employee:

1. Is assigned or

2. Reports. 29 C.F.R. §§ 825.106, 825.111(a)(3).

The employee is also counted by the secondary employer to determine eligibility for the secondary employer's full-time or permanent employees. 29 C.F.R. §§ 825.106, 825.111(a)(3).

i. Seventy-five Mile Distance

The seventy-five mile distance is measured by surface miles, using surface transportation by the shortest route from the facility where the eligible employee needing FMLA leave is employed, over:

1. Public streets;

2. Roads;

3. Highways; and

4. Waterways. 29 C.F.R. § 825.111(b).

Absent available surface transportation between worksites, the distance is measured by using the most frequently utilized mode of transportation, for example, airline miles.

j. Number of Employees

The determination of how many employees are employed within seventy-five miles of the worksite of an employee is based on the number of employees maintained on the payroll. 29 C.F.R. § 825.111(c). Employees of educational institutions who are employed permanently or who are under contract are "maintained on the payroll" during any portion of the year when school is not in session. 29 C.F.R. § 825.111(c).

D. LEAVE AMOUNT

An eligible employee's FMLA leave entitlement is limited to a total of twelve workweeks of leave during any twelve month period. 29 U.S.C.A. § 2612(a); 29 C.F.R. § 825.200.

1. THE TWELVE MONTH PERIOD

An employer is permitted to choose any one of the following methods for determining the twelve month period in which the twelve weeks of FMLA leave entitlement occurs:

1. The calendar year;
2. Any fixed twelve month "leave year," such as a:
   a. Fiscal year;
   b. Year required by state law; or
   c. Year starting on an employee's "anniversary" date;
3. The twelve month period measured forward from the date any employee's first FMLA leave begins; or
4. A "rolling" twelve month period measured backward from the date an employee uses any FMLA leave, except that this measure may not extend back before August 5, 1993. 29 C.F.R. § 825.200(b).

2. SELECTION OF THE TWELVE
MONTH PERIOD

Employers may choose any one of the alternatives provided the alternative selected is applied consistently and uniformly to all employees. 29 C.F.R. § 825.200(d)1). If an employer fails to select one of the options for measuring the twelve month period, the option that provides the most beneficial outcome for the employee is used.

3. CHANGING THE TWELVE
MONTH PERIOD

An employer wishing to change to another alternative is required to give at least sixty days notice to all employees. 29 C.F.R. § 825.200(d)(1). The transition must take place in a way that the employees retain the full benefit of twelve weeks of FMLA leave under whichever method affords the greatest benefit to the employee.

4. CALCULATING THE AMOUNT
OF LEAVE

For purposes of determining the amount of leave used by an employee, the fact that a holiday may occur within the week taken as FMLA leave has no effect. 29 C.F.R. § 825.200(f). The week is counted as a week of FMLA leave. However, if for some reason the employer's business activity has temporarily ceased and employees generally are not expected to report for work for one or more weeks, for example, a school closing two weeks for the Christmas/New Year holiday or the summer vacation or an employer closing the plant for retooling or repairs, the days the employers' activities have ceased do not count against the employee's FMLA leave entitlement.

5. EXPIRATION OF LEAVE FOR THE BIRTH OF A CHILD, OR FOR PLACEMENT OF A CHILD FOR ADOPTION OR FOSTER CARE

An employee's entitlement to leave for a birth or placement for adoption or foster care expires at the end of the twelve month period beginning on the date of the birth or placement, unless state law allows, or the employer permits, leave to be taken for a longer period. 29 C.F.R. § 825.201. The FMLA leave must be included within this one-year period.

6. HUSBAND AND WIFE LEAVE ENTITLEMENTS

A husband and wife who are eligible for FMLA leave and are employed by the same employer may be limited to a combined total of twelve weeks of leave during any twelve month period if the leave is taken:

1. For birth of the employee's daughter or son or to care for the child after birth;

2. For placement of a daughter or son with the employee for adoption or foster care, or to care for the child after placement; or

3. To care for the employee's parent with a
    serious health condition. 29 U.S.C.A.
    § 2612(f); 29 C.F.R. § 825.202.

This limitation on the total weeks of leave applies
to leave taken for the reasons specified in the
FMLA as long as a husband and wife are employed
by the "same employer." 29 C.F.R. § 825.202(b). It
would apply even though the spouses are employed:

1. At two different worksites of an employer
    located more than seventy-five miles from
    each other or

2. By two different operating divisions of the
    same employer. 29 C.F.R. § 825.202(b).

However, if one spouse is ineligible for FMLA leave,
the other spouse would be entitled to a full twelve
weeks of FMLA leave. 29 C.F.R. § 825.202(b).

Where the husband and wife both use a portion of
the total twelve week FMLA leave entitlement for
one of the permitted FMLA purposes, the husband
and wife would each be entitled to the difference
between the amount he or she has taken individually and twelve weeks for FMLA leave for a purpose
other than that contained above. 29 C.F.R.
§ 825.202(c). For example, if each spouse took six
weeks of leave to care for a healthy, newborn child,
each could use an additional six weeks:

1. Due to his or her own serious health condi-
    tion or

2. To care for a child or parent with a serious
    health condition.

Many state pregnancy disability laws specify a period of disability either before or after a child's birth. 29 C.F.R. § 825.202(c). These periods would also be considered FMLA leave for a serious health condition of the mother, and would not be subject to the combined limit.

E. PAID OR UNPAID LEAVE

Generally, FMLA leave is unpaid. 29 U.S.C.A. § 2612(c); 29 C.F.R. § 825.207(a). However, the FMLA permits an eligible employee to choose to substitute paid leave for FMLA leave. 29 U.S.C.A. § 2612(d)(2); 29 C.F.R. § 825.207(a). If an employee does not choose to substitute accrued paid leave, the employer may require the employee to substitute accrued paid leave for FMLA leave. 29 U.S.C.A. § 2612(d)(2); 29 C.F.R. § 825.207(a).

1. FAMILY LEAVE

The FMLA's term "family leave" refers to paid leave provided by the employer covering the particular circumstances for which the employee seeks leave for either the:

1. Birth of a child and to care for this child;

2. Placement of a child for adoption or foster care; or

3. Care for a spouse, child, or parent with a serious health condition. 29 C.F.R. § 825.207(b).

For example, if the employer's leave plan allows use of family leave to care for a child but not for a parent, the employer is not required to allow accrued family leave to be substituted for FMLA leave used to care for a parent.

2.   VACATION, PERSONAL, OR MEDICAL/SICK LEAVE

Substitution of paid accrued vacation, personal, or medical/sick leave may be made for any unpaid FMLA leave needed to:

1. Care for a family member or
2. The employee's own serious health condition. 29 C.F.R. § 825.207(c).

Paid vacation or personal leave, including leave earned or accrued under plans allowing paid time off, may be substituted, at either the employee's or the employer's option, for any qualified FMLA leave. 29 C.F.R. § 825.207(e). No limitations may be placed by the employer on substitution of paid vacation or personal leave for these purposes. 29 C.F.R. § 825.207(e).

Substitution of paid sick/medical leave may be elected to the extent the circumstances meet the employer's usual requirements for the use of sick/medical leave. 29 C.F.R. § 825.207(c). An employer is not required to allow substitution of paid sick or medical leave for unpaid FMLA leave in any situation where the employer's uniform policy would not normally allow this paid leave. 29 C.F.R.

§ 825.207(c). An employee, has a right to substitute paid medical/sick leave to care for a seriously ill family member only if the employer's leave plan allows paid leave to be used for that purpose. 29 C.F.R. § 825.207(c). Similarly, an employee does not have a right to substitute paid medical/sick leave for a serious health condition which is not covered by the employer's leave plan. 29 C.F.R. § 825.207(c).

3. DISABILITY LEAVE

Disability leave for a child's birth would be considered FMLA leave for a serious health condition and counted in the twelve weeks of leave permitted. 29 C.F.R. § 825.207(d)(1). Because the leave pursuant to a temporary disability benefit plan is not unpaid, the provision for substitution of paid leave is inapplicable. However, the employer may designate the leave as FMLA leave and count the leave as running concurrently for purposes of both the:

1. Benefit plan and

2. FMLA leave entitlement. 29 C.F.R. § 825.207(d)(1).

If the requirements to qualify for payments pursuant to the employer's temporary disability plan are more stringent than those of the FMLA, the employee:

1. Must meet the plan's more stringent requirements or

2. May choose not to meet the requirements of the plan and instead:

i. Receive no payments from the plan and

ii. Use unpaid FMLA leave or substitute available accrued paid leave. 29 C.F.R. § 825.207(d)(1).

4. WORKERS' COMPENSATION

The employee or the employer may choose to have the employee's FMLA twelve week leave entitlement run concurrently with a workers' compensation absence when the injury is one that meets the criteria for a serious health condition. 29 C.F.R. § 825.207(d)(2). Because the workers' compensation absence is not unpaid leave, the provision for substitution of the employee's accrued paid leave is not applicable. However, if the health care provider treating the employee for the worker's compensation injury certifies that the employee is able to return to a light duty job but is unable to return to the same or equivalent job, the employee may decline the employer's offer of a light duty job. As a result, the employee may lose workers' compensation payments, but is entitled to remain on unpaid FMLA leave until the twelve week entitlement is exhausted. On the date the workers' compensation benefits cease, the substitution provision becomes applicable and either the employee may elect or the employer may require the use of accrued paid leave.

5. FAILURE OF EMPLOYEE OR EMPLOYER TO ELECT TO SUBSTITUTE PAID LEAVE

If neither the employee nor the employer elects to substitute paid leave for unpaid FMLA leave, the employee will remain entitled to all the paid leave which is earned or accrued under the terms of the employer's plan. 29 C.F.R. § 825.207(f).

When an employee or employer elects to substitute paid leave of any type for unpaid FMLA leave under circumstances permitted and the employer's procedural requirements for taking that kind of leave are less stringent than the FMLA's requirements, for example, notice or certification requirements, only the less stringent requirements may be imposed. 29 C.F.R. § 825.207(h). An employee who complies with an employer's less stringent leave plan requirements may not have leave for an FMLA purpose delayed or denied on the grounds that the employee has not complied with the FMLA's stricter requirements. However, where accrued paid vacation or personal leave is substituted for unpaid FMLA leave for a serious health condition, an employee may be required to comply with any less stringent medical certification requirements of the employer's sick leave program. 29 C.F.R. § 825.207(h).

6. PAID LEAVE THAT DOES NOT COUNT AS FMLA LEAVE

If an employee uses paid leave under circumstances which do not qualify as FMLA leave, the leave will not count against the twelve weeks of FMLA leave to which the employee is entitled. 29 C.F.R. § 825.207(g). For example, paid sick leave used for a medical condition which is not a serious health condition does not count as an FMLA leave.

7. PUBLIC EMPLOYEES USE OF COMPENSATORY TIME

The Fair Labor Standards Act (FLSA) permits public employers under prescribed circumstances to substitute compensatory time off accrued at one and one-half hours for each overtime hour worked in lieu of paying cash to an employee when the employee works overtime hours. 29 C.F.R. § 825.207(i). There are limits to the compensatory time hours that an employee may accumulate depending upon whether the employee works:

1. In fire protection or law enforcement (480 hours) or

2. Elsewhere for a public agency (240 hours).

Compensatory time off is not a form of accrued paid leave that an employer may require the employee to substitute for unpaid FMLA leave. The employee may request to use his or her balance of compensatory time for an FMLA reason. If the employer permits the accrual to be used in compliance with the FLSA's regulations, the absence which is paid from the employee's accrued compensatory time account may not be counted against the employee's FMLA leave entitlement. 29 C.F.R. § 825.207(i); see also 29 C.F.R. § 553.25.

8. EMPLOYER DESIGNATION OF LEAVE—PAID OR UNPAID

It is the employer's responsibility to designate leave, paid or unpaid, as FMLA-qualifying, and to give notice of the designation to the employee. 29 C.F.R. § 825.208(a). For intermittent leave or leave on a reduced schedule, only one notice is required unless the circumstances regarding the leave have changed.

The employer's designation decision must be based only on information received from the employee or the employee's spokesperson. For example, if the employee is incapacitated, the employee's spouse, adult child, parent, doctor, etc., may provide notice to the employer of the need to take FMLA leave. Where the employer does not have sufficient information about the reason for an employee's use of paid leave, the employer should inquire further of the employee or the spokesperson to ascertain whether the paid leave is FMLA-qualifying.

An employee giving notice for FMLA leave must explain the reasons for the leave to allow the employer to determine that the leave qualifies. 29

C.F.R. § 825.208(a)(1). If the employee fails to explain the reasons, leave may be denied.

An employee giving notice of the need for unpaid FMLA leave does not need to expressly assert FMLA rights or even mention the FMLA to meet his or her obligation to provide notice. The employee, however, must state a qualifying reason for the leave. 29 C.F.R. §§ 825.208(a)(2), 825.302(c).

If an employee requesting to use paid leave for an FMLA purpose does not explain the leave's reason, and the employer denies the employee's request, the employee must provide sufficient information to establish an FMLA qualifying reason; i.e., that the leave may not be denied. 29 C.F.R. § 825.208(a)(2). Similarly, an employee using accrued paid vacation leave who seeks an extension of unpaid leave for an FMLA qualifying purpose must state the reason. 29 C.F.R. § 825.208(a)(2). If this is due to an event which occurred during the paid leave's period, the employer may count the leave used after the FMLA qualifying event against the employee's twelve week entitlement.

Once the employer has acquired knowledge that the leave is for an FMLA required reason, the employer must promptly within two business days, absent extenuating circumstances, notify the employee that the paid leave is designated and will be counted as FMLA leave. 29 C.F.R. § 825.208(b)(1). If there is a dispute between an employer and an employee whether paid leave qualifies as FMLA leave, it should be resolved through discussions between the employee and the employer. These discussions and the decision must be documented.

The employer's notice to the employee that the leave has been designated as FMLA leave may:

1. Be oral or

2. In writing. 29 C.F.R. § 825.208(b)(2).

If the notice is oral, it must be confirmed in writing, no later than the following payday unless the payday is less than one week after the oral notice, in which case the notice must be no later than the subsequent payday. The written notice may be in any form, including a notation on the employee's pay stub.

If the employer requires paid leave to be substituted for unpaid leave, or that paid leave taken under an existing leave plan be counted as FMLA leave, this decision must be made by the employer within two business days of the time the employee gives notice of the leave, or, where the employer does not initially have sufficient information to make a determination, when the employer determines that the leave qualifies as FMLA leave. 29 C.F.R. § 825.208(c). The employer's designation must be made before the leave starts, unless the employer does not have sufficient information as to the employee's reason for taking the leave until after the leave commenced. 29 C.F.R. § 825.208(c).

If the employer has the requisite knowledge to make a determination that the paid leave is for an FMLA reason when the employee gives notice for leave or commences leave and fails to designate the leave as FMLA leave and so notifies the employee, the employer may not designate the leave as FMLA retroactively, and may designate only prospectively as of the date of notification to the employee of the designation. 29 C.F.R. § 825.208(c). In these circumstances, the employee is subject to the FMLA's full protections, but none of the absences preceding the notice to the employee of the designation may be counted against the employee's twelve week FMLA leave entitlement.

If the employer learns that leave is for an FMLA purpose after leave has begun, such as when an employee gives notice for an extension of the paid leave with unpaid FMLA leave, the entire or some portion of the paid leave may be retroactively counted as FMLA leave, to the extent that it qualifies as FMLA leave. 29 C.F.R. § 825.208(d). For example, an employee is granted two weeks paid vacation leave for a skiing trip. In mid-week of the second week, the employee contacts the employer for a leave extension as unpaid leave and advises that at the beginning of the second week of paid vacation leave the employee suffered a severe accident requiring hospitalization. The employer may notify the employee that the extension and the second week of paid vacation leave from the injury's date is FMLA leave.

When the employee takes sick leave that turns into a serious health condition (for example, bronchitis that turns into bronchial pneumonia) and the employee gives notice for a leave extension, the entire period of the serious health condition may be counted as FMLA leave. 29 C.F.R. § 825.208(d).

Employers may not designate leave as FMLA leave after the employee has returned to work with two exceptions:

1. If the employee was absent for an FMLA reason and the employer did not learn the reason for the absence until the employee's return (for example, where the employee was absent for only a brief period), the employer may, upon the employee's return to work, promptly within two business days of the employee's return to work designate the leave retroactively with appropriate notice to the employee. If leave is taken for an FMLA reason and has not been so designated by the employer, but the employee desires that the leave be counted as FMLA leave, the employee must notify the employer within two business days of returning to work that the leave was for an FMLA reason. In the absence of this timely notification by the employee, the employee may not subsequently assert FMLA protections for the absence.

2. If the employer knows the reason for the leave but has not been able to confirm that the leave qualifies under the FMLA, or where the employer has requested medical certification which has not yet been received or the parties are in the process of obtaining a second or third medical opinion, the employer

should make a preliminary designation, and so notify the employee, at the time leave begins, or as soon as the reason for the leave becomes known. Upon receipt of the requisite information from the employee or of the medical certification which confirms the leave is for an FMLA reason, the preliminary designation becomes final. If the medical certifications fail to confirm that the reason for the absence was an FMLA reason, the employer must withdraw the designation with written notice to the employee. 29 C.F.R. § 825.208(e).

NOTE: The above FMLA regulations have been challenged and in certain federal court circuits may be invalid. See *Cox v. Autozone, Inc.*, 990 F.Supp. 1369 (M.D.Ala.1998) (the FMLA's regulations convert an employer's statutory right to require an employee to substitute employer-provided paid leave for unpaid FMLA leave into an employee entitlement to more than twelve weeks of leave); *Seaman v. Downtown Partnership*, 991 F.Supp. 751 (D.Md.1998) (this regulation contradicts Congress' intent regarding employee eligibility; i.e, if the employee is ineligible for FMLA leave, the employer cannot on its own action confer statutory FMLA status on the employee); *Wolke v. Dreadnought Marine, Inc.*, 954 F.Supp. 1133 (E.D.Va.1997) (the Department of Labor (DOL) usurped the legislature's and judiciary's constitutional authority in making an employee eligible for FMLA leave unless the employee is given notice of ineligibility from the employer within two days after it receives the employee's leave request).

F. INTERMITTENT OR REDUCED LEAVE SCHEDULE

Under certain circumstances, FMLA leave may be taken intermittently or on a reduced leave schedule. 29 U.S.C.A. § 2612(b).

1. INTERMITTENT LEAVE—DEFINITION

Intermittent leave is FMLA leave taken in separate blocks of time due to a single qualifying reason. 29 C.F.R. § 825.203(a).

2. REDUCED LEAVE SCHEDULE—DEFINITION

A reduced leave schedule is a leave schedule that reduces an employee's usual number of working hours per workweek, or hours per workday. 29 C.F.R. § 825.203(a). A reduced leave schedule is a change in the employee's schedule for a period of time, normally from full-time to part-time.

3. INTERMITTENT LEAVE—BIRTH OR PLACEMENT OF A CHILD FOR ADOPTION OR FOSTER CARE

When leave is taken after a child's birth or placement for adoption or foster care, an employee may take leave intermittently or on a reduced leave schedule only if the employer agrees. 29 C.F.R. § 825.204(b). A schedule reduction might occur, for example, where an employee and employer agree to part-time work after the child's birth or the leave is taken in several segments. The employer's agreement is not required, however, for leave during which the mother has a serious health condition in connection with the child's birth or if the newborn child has a serious health condition.

4. INTERMITTENT LEAVE—SERIOUS HEALTH CONDITION

Leave may be taken intermittently or on a reduced leave schedule when medically necessary for:

1. Planned and/or unanticipated medical treatment of a related serious health condition by or under the supervision of a health care provider;

2. Recovery from treatment or recovery from a serious health condition; or

3. Care or psychological comfort to an immediate family member with a serious health condition. 29 C.F.R. § 825.204(c).

Intermittent leave may be taken for a serious health condition which requires treatment by a health care provider periodically, rather than for one continuous time period. It may include leave periods from an hour or more to several weeks. 29 C.F.R. § 825.204(c)(1). Examples of intermittent leave include:

1. Leave taken on an occasional basis for medical appointments or

2. Leave taken several days at a time over a six month period, for example, for chemotherapy. 29 C.F.R. § 825.204(c)(1).

A pregnant employee may take leave intermittently for prenatal examinations or for her own condition, such as for periods of severe morning sickness. 29 C.F.R. § 825.204(c)(1).

An example of an employee taking leave on a reduced leave schedule is an employee who is recovering from a serious health condition and is not strong enough to work a full-time schedule.

5. INTERMITTENT LEAVE—EMPLOYEE'S OR FAMILY MEMBER'S SERIOUS HEALTH CONDITION

Intermittent or reduced schedule leave may be taken for absences where the employee or family member is incapacitated or unable to perform the position's essential functions because of a chronic serious health condition even if he or she does not receive treatment by a health care provider. 29 C.F.R. § 825.204(c)(2).

6. INTERMITTENT LEAVE INCREMENTS

There is no limit on the size of an increment of leave when an employee takes intermittent leave or leave on a reduced leave schedule. 29 C.F.R. § 825.204(d). The employer may limit leave increments to the shortest time period that the employer's payroll system uses to account for absences or use of leave, provided it is one hour or less. 29 C.F.R. § 825.204(d). For example, an employee might take two hours off for a medical appointment, or might work a reduced day of four hours over a period of several weeks while recuperating from an illness. An employee may not be required to take more FMLA leave than necessary to address the circumstance that precipitated the leave's need.

7. ALTERNATIVE POSITION AND TRANSFER

The employer may require the employee to transfer temporarily, during the intermittent or reduced leave schedule's time period, to an available alternative position:

1. For which the employee is qualified;

2. Which better accommodates recurring periods of leave than does the employee's regular position for which the employee is qualified; and

3. Which better accommodates recurring periods of leave than does the employee's regular position if:

    a. An employee needs intermittent leave or leave on a reduced leave schedule that is foreseeable based on planned medical treatment for the employee or a family member, including during a period of recovery from a serious health condition or

b. The employer agrees to permit intermittent or reduced schedule leave for a child's birth, placement for adoption, or foster care. 29 U.S.C.A. § 2612(b)(2); 29 C.F.R. § 825.204.

Transfer to an alternative position may require compliance with any applicable collective bargaining agreement, federal law (for example, the Americans with Disabilities Act (ADA)), and state law. 29 C.F.R. § 825.204(b). Transfer to an alternative position may include altering an existing job to better accommodate the employee's need for intermittent or reduced leave.

The alternative position must have equivalent:

1. Pay and

2. Benefits. 29 C.F.R. § 825.204(c).

An alternative position for these purposes does not have to have equivalent duties. 29 C.F.R. § 825.204(c).

The employer may increase the pay and benefits of an existing alternative position to make them equivalent to the pay and benefits of the employee's regular job. 29 C.F.R. § 825.204(c). The employer may also transfer the employee to a part-time job with the same hourly pay rate and benefits, provided the employee is not required to take more leave than is medically necessary. 29 C.F.R. § 825.204(c). For example, an employee desiring to take leave in increments of four hours per day could be transferred to a half-time job, or could remain in the employee's same job on a part-time schedule, paying the same hourly rate as the employee's previous job and enjoying the same benefits.

The employer may not eliminate benefits which otherwise would not be provided to part-time employees. 29 C.F.R. § 825.204(c). An employer may proportionately reduce benefits such as vacation leave where an employer's normal practice is to base these benefits on the number of hours worked. 29 C.F.R. § 825.204(c).

An employer may not transfer the employee to an alternative position to discourage the employee from:

1.   Taking FMLA leave or

2.   Otherwise work a hardship on the employee. 29 C.F.R. § 825.204(d).

For example, an employer may not:

1.   Assign a white collar employee laborer's work;

2.   Reassign an employee working the day shift to the graveyard shift; or

3.   Reassign an employee working in the headquarters facility to a branch a significant distance away from the employee's normal job location.

Attempts on the employer's part to make this type of transfer would violate the FMLA.

8. CALCULATION OF INTERMITTENT LEAVE USED

If an employee takes leave on an intermittent or reduced leave schedule, only the amount of leave actually taken may be counted toward the FMLA leave to which an employee is entitled. 29 C.F.R. § 825.205(a). For example, if an employee who normally works five days a week takes off one day, the employee would use one fifth of a week of FMLA leave. Similarly, if a full-time employee who normally works eight hour days works four hour days under a reduced leave schedule, the employee would use one half week of FMLA leave each week.

Where an employee normally works a part-time schedule or variable hours, the amount of leave to which an employee is entitled is determined on a pro rata or proportional basis by comparing the new schedule with the employee's normal work schedule. 29 C.F.R. § 825.205(b). For example, if an employee who normally works thirty hours per week works only twenty hours a week under a reduced leave schedule, the employee's ten hours of leave would constitute one-third of week of FMLA leave for each week the employee works the reduced leave schedule.

If an employer has made a permanent or long-term change in the employee's schedule for reasons other than the FMLA, and prior to the notice for FMLA leave, the hours worked under the new schedule are to be used for making this calculation.

29 C.F.R. § 825.205(c). If an employee's schedule varies from week to week, a weekly average of the hours worked over the twelve weeks prior to the beginning of the leave period are used for calculating the employee's normal workweek. 29 C.F.R. § 825.205(d).

9. DEDUCTIONS FROM PAY

a. Salaried Executive, Administrative, or Professional Employees

If an employee is otherwise exempt from minimum wage and overtime requirements of the Fair Labor Standards Act (FLSA) as a salaried executive, administrative, or professional employee, providing unpaid FMLA-qualifying leave to this employee will not cause the employee to lose the FLSA exemption. 29 C.F.R. § 825.206(a); see also 29 C.F.R. Part 541. This means that under the FLSA's regulations that when an employee meets the specified duties test, is paid on a salary basis, and is paid a salary of at least the amount specified in the regulations, the employer may make deductions from the employee's salary for any hours taken as intermittent or reduced FMLA leave within a workweek, without affecting the employee's exempt status.

b. Fluctuating Workweek

For an employee paid in accordance with the FLSA's fluctuating workweek payment method for overtime, the employer, during the period in which intermittent or reduced schedule FMLA leave is scheduled to be taken, may compensate an employee on an hourly basis and pay only for the hours the employee works, including time and one-half the employee's regular rate for overtime hours. 29 C.F.R. § 825.206(b); see also 29 C.F.R. § 778.114. The change to payment on an hourly basis would include the entire period during which the employee is taking intermittent leave, including weeks in which no leave is taken.

The hourly rate would be determined by dividing the employee's weekly salary by the employee's normal or average schedule of hours worked during weeks in which FMLA leave is not being taken. If an employer chooses to follow this exception from the fluctuating workweek payment method, the employer must do so uniformly, with respect to all employees paid on a fluctuating workweek basis for whom FMLA leave is taken on an intermittent or reduced leave schedule basis. If an employer does not elect to convert the employee's compensation to hourly pay, no deduction may be taken for the FMLA leave. Once the need for intermittent or reduced scheduled leave is over, the employee may be restored to payment on a fluctuating work week basis.

10. EMPLOYEE'S RIGHTS UPON INTERMITTENT OR REDUCED LEAVE SCHEDULE'S END

When an employee who is taking leave intermittently or on a reduced leave schedule and has been transferred to an alternative position, no longer needs to continue on leave and is able to return to full-time work, the employee must be placed in the same or equivalent job as the job he or she left when the leave commenced. 29 C.F.R. § 825.204(e). An employee may not be required to take more leave than necessary to address the circumstance that precipitated the leave's need.

G. BENEFIT CONTINUATION

1. EMPLOYER'S RESPONSIBILITY TO MAINTAIN BENEFITS FOR EMPLOYEES ON LEAVE

During any FMLA leave, an employer must maintain the employee's coverage under any group health plan. 29 U.S.C.A. § 2614(c); 29 C.F.R. § 825.209. The employee's coverage must be maintained by the employer on the same conditions as coverage would have been provided if the employee had been continuously employed during the entire FMLA leave.

For the FMLA's purposes, a group health plan is as defined in the Internal Revenue Code of 1986. See 26 U.S.C.A. § 5000(b)(1). It means a plan, including a self-insured plan, of, or contributed to by an employer (including a self-employed person) or employee organization to provide health care, directly or otherwise, to:

1. Employees;

2. Former employees;

3. The employer; or

4. Others associated or formerly associated with the employer in a business relationship. 26 U.S.C.A. § 5000(b)(1).

2. EFFECT OF EMPLOYER'S PROVIDING NEW BENEFITS WHILE AN EMPLOYEE IS ON FMLA LEAVE

If an employer provides a new group health plan benefit or changes health plan benefits to the employee's advantage while an employee is on FMLA leave, the employee is entitled to:

1. The new or changed plan benefits and

2. These benefits must be provided to the same extent as if the employee were not on leave. 29 C.F.R. § 825.209(c).

For example, if an employer changes a group health benefit plan to provide dental care, an employee on FMLA leave must be given the same opportunity as other employees to receive or obtain the dental care coverage. Any other plan content changes, for example, in coverage, deductibles, etc., which apply to all employees of the workforce would also apply to an employee on FMLA leave; provided they are:

1. Advantageous to the employee on leave and

2. Do not decrease any existing benefit. 29 C.F.R. § 825.209(c).

3. NOTICE OF OPPORTUNITY TO CHANGE BENEFIT COVERAGE

Notice of any opportunity to change group health plan benefits must be given to an employee on FMLA leave. 29 C.F.R. 825.209(d). For example, if the group health plan permits an employee to change from single to family coverage upon a child's birth or otherwise add new family members, this change in benefits must be made available while an employee is on FMLA leave. If the employee requests the changed coverage, it must be provided by the employer.

4. EMPLOYEE'S OPTION TO FOREGO BENEFITS WHILE ON FMLA LEAVE

An employee may choose not to retain group health plan benefit coverage during an FMLA leave. 29 C.F.R. § 825.209(e). However, when an employee returns from leave, the employee is entitled to be reinstated:

1. With the same group health plan benefits as existed prior to taking the leave and

2. Without any qualifying period, physical examination, exclusion of pre-existing conditions, etc., including eligibility for family or dependent coverages.

For example, an employee may elect not to continue his or her share of payments for a group health plan's benefits while on an FMLA leave because of cost. The employer, however, may still desire to continue these benefits at its cost to ensure that upon the employee's return to work that:

1. The same group health plan benefits as existed prior to taking the leave exist and

2. No new qualifying period, physical examination, exclusion of pre-existing conditions, etc., including eligibility for family or dependent coverages exists. See 29 C.F.R. § 825.212(c).

Should this occur, the employer can recover the cost of the benefits paid on the employee's behalf when the employee returns from FMLA leave. 29 C.F.R. § 825.212(b). Likewise, if the employee fails to return from the FMLA leave, the employer can recover the costs of the benefits it paid on the employee's behalf, unless the reason that the employee does not return is due to:

1. The continuation, recurrence, or onset of a serious health condition of the employee or the employee's family member which would otherwise entitle the employee to FMLA leave or

2. Other circumstances beyond the employee's control, including where:

   a. A parent chooses to stay home with a newborn child who has a serious health condition;

   b. An employee's spouse is unexpectedly transferred to a job location more than seventy-five miles from the employee's worksite;

c. A relative or individual other than an immediate family member has a serious health condition and the employee is needed to provide care;

d. The employee is laid off while on leave; or

e. The employee is a "key employee" who decides not to return to work upon being notified of the employer's intention to deny restoration because of substantial and grievous economic injury to the employer's operations and is not reinstated by the employer. 29 U.S.C.A. § 2614(c)(2); 29 C.F.R. § 825.213(a).

5. DISCONTINUATION OF BENEFITS AFTER AN FMLA LEAVE

Except as required by the Consolidated Omnibus Budget Reconciliation Act of 1986 (COBRA) and for "key" employees, an employer's obligation to maintain group health plan benefits during an FMLA leave and to restore the employee to the same or equivalent employment under the FMLA ceases:

1. If the employment relationship would have terminated even if the employee had not taken FMLA leave, for example, if the employee's position was eliminated as part of a nondiscriminatory reduction in force and the employee would not have been transferred to another position;

2. An employee informs the employer of his or her intent not to return from leave, including before starting the leave if the employer is so informed before the leave begins; or

3. The employee fails to return from leave or continues on leave after exhausting his or her FMLA leave entitlement in the twelve month period. 29 C.F.R. § 825.209(f).

If a "key employee" does not return from an FMLA leave when notified by the employer that substantial or grievous economic injury will result from his or her reinstatement, the employee's entitlement to group health plan benefits:

1. Continues unless and until the employee advises the employer that the employee does not desire restoration to employment at the end of the leave period or

2. The FMLA leave entitlement is exhausted or reinstatement is actually denied. 29 C.F.R. §§ 825.209(g), 825.218.

6. ENTITLEMENT TO OTHER THAN GROUP HEALTH PLAN BENEFITS

An employee may be entitled to other than group health plan benefits while on an FMLA leave. 29 C.F.R. § 825.209(h). If the employee is entitled to these benefits, they must be provided during the FMLA leave. For example, if holiday pay is granted by the employer's established policy to employees on other forms of leave (paid or unpaid), it must be provided to employees on FMLA leave.

7. EMPLOYEE'S PAYMENT OF BENEFITS WHILE ON LEAVE

a. Employee's Share of Benefit Payment

Any share of group health plan premiums which had been paid by the employee prior to the FMLA leave must continue to be paid by the employee during the FMLA leave. 29 C.F.R. § 825.210(a). If premiums are raised or lowered, the employee must pay the new premium rates.

b. Employee's Share of Premiums—Substituted Paid Leave

If the FMLA leave is substituted paid leave, the employee's share of the premiums must be paid by the method normally used during any paid leave, presumably as a payroll deduction. 29 C.F.R. § 825.210(b).

c. Employee's Share of Premiums—Unpaid Leave

If FMLA leave is unpaid, the employer has a number of options for obtaining payment from the employee. 29 C.F.R. 825.210(c). The employer may require that payment be made to:

1. The employer or

2. The insurance carrier.

However, the employer may not add to the employee's premium a payment for administrative expenses. 29 C.F.R. § 825.210(c).

d. Method of Premium Payment

The employer must provide the employee with advance written notice of the terms and conditions under which these premium payments must be made. 29 C.F.R. §§ 825.210(d), 825.301. An employer may require employees to pay their premium payment share as follows:

1. Payment can be due at the same time as it would be made if by payroll deduction;

2. Payment can be due on the same schedule as payments are made under COBRA;

3. Payment can be prepaid pursuant to a cafeteria plan at the employee's option;

4. The employer's existing rules for payment by employees on "leave without pay" can be followed, provided that these rules do not require:

   a. Prepayment, for example, prior to the leave's commencement, of the premiums that wi'l become due during the unpaid FMLA leave or

   b. Payment of higher premiums than if the employee had continued to work instead of taking leave.

5. Another system voluntarily agreed to between the employer and the employee, which may

include prepayment of premiums, for example, through increased payroll deductions when the need for FMLA leave is foreseeable. 29 C.F.R. § 825.210(c).

An employer may not require more of an employee using FMLA leave than the employer requires of other employees on any other "leave without pay." 29 C.F.R. § 825.210(e).

e. Employee's Failure to Make Timely Health Plan Premium Payments

In the absence of an established employer policy providing a longer grace period, an employer's FMLA obligations to maintain group health insurance coverage cease if an employee's premium payment is more than thirty days late. 29 C.F.R. § 825.212(a)(1). To terminate the coverage, the employer must provide written notice to the employee that the payment has not been received. This notice must:

1. Be mailed to the employee at least fifteen days before coverage is to cease and

2. Advise the employee that coverage will be terminated on a specified date at least fifteen days after the date of the letter unless the payment has been received by that date. 29 C.F.R. § 825.212(a)(1).

If the employer has established policies regarding other forms of unpaid leave that provide for the employer to cease coverage retroactively to the date the unpaid premium payment was due, the employer may terminate the employee's coverage retroactively in accordance with that policy, provided the fifteen day notice was given. In the absence of this policy, coverage for the employee may be terminated at the end of the thirty day grace period, where the required fifteen day notice has been provided. 29 C.F.R. § 825.212(a)(1).

8. MAINTENANCE OF NON–GROUP HEALTH INSURANCE

Maintenance of group health insurance policies which are not a part of the employer's group health plan, are the employee's sole responsibility. 29 C.F.R. §§ 825.209(a), 825.210, 825.212(a)(2). The employer should notify the employee to make necessary arrangements with the insurer for these premiums' payment during the FMLA leave or have coverage discontinued.

9. WORKERS' COMPENSATION PAYMENTS

An employee who is receiving payments due to a workers' compensation injury must make arrangements with the employer for payment of group health plan benefits when simultaneously taking unpaid FMLA leave. 29 C.F.R. §§ 825.207(d)(2), 825.210(f).

10. MULTI–EMPLOYER HEALTH PLANS

A multi-employer health plan is a plan to which more than one employer is required to contribute, and which is maintained pursuant to one or more collective bargaining agreements between employee organization(s) and the employers. 29 C.F.R. § 825.211(a). An employer under a multi-employer plan must continue to make contributions on behalf of an employee using FMLA leave as though the employee had been continuously employed, unless the plan contains an explicit FMLA provision for maintaining coverage such as through pooled contributions by all employers party to the plan. 29 C.F.R. § 825.211(b).

During the employee's FMLA leave, coverage by the group health plan, and benefits provided pursuant to the plan, must be maintained at the level of coverage and benefits which were applicable to the employee at the time the FMLA leave commenced. 29 C.F.R. § 825.211(c). An employee using FMLA leave cannot be required to use banked hours or pay a greater premium than the employee would have been required to pay if the employee had been continuously employed. 29 C.F.R. § 825.211(d).

11. EMPLOYER'S VOLUNTARY CONTINUATION OF OTHER BENEFITS

Under some circumstances, an employer may elect to maintain other benefits, for example, life insurance, disability insurance, etc., by paying the employee's share of premiums during the unpaid FMLA leave. 29 C.F.R. § 825.213(b). This may be done to ensure that the employer can meet its responsibilities to provide equivalent benefits to the employee upon return from unpaid FMLA leave by paying premiums to avoid a lapse of coverage. If the employer elects to maintain these benefits during the leave, at the conclusion of leave, the employer is entitled to recover only the costs incurred for paying the employee's share of any premiums whether or not the employee returns to work. 29 C.F.R. § 825.213(b).

12. RECOVERY OF EMPLOYER'S BENEFIT PAYMENTS FOR EMPLOYEE'S FAILURE TO RETURN TO WORK

a. **Employer's Recovery of Benefit Payments**

An employer may recover its share of group health plan premiums during a period of unpaid FMLA leave from an employee if the employee fails to return to work after the employee's FMLA leave entitlement has been exhausted or expires, unless the reason the employee does not return is due to:

1. The continuation, recurrence, or onset of a serious health condition of the employee or the employee's family member which would otherwise entitle the employee to leave under the FMLA or

2. Other circumstances beyond the employee's control, including where:

a. A parent chooses to stay home with a new-born child who has a serious health condition;

b. An employee's spouse is unexpectedly transferred to a job location more than seventy-five miles from the employee's worksite;

c. A relative or individual other than an immediate family member has a serious health condition and the employee is needed to provide care;

d. The employee is laid off while on leave; or

e. The employee is a "key employee" who decides not to return to work upon being notified of the employer's intention to deny restoration because of substantial and grievous economic injury to the employer's operations and is not reinstated by the employer. 29 C.F.R. § 825.213(a).

Other circumstances beyond the employee's control would not include a situation where:

a. An employee desires to remain with a parent in a distant city even though the parent no longer requires the employee's care or

b. A parent chooses not to return to work to stay home with a well, newborn child. 29 C.F.R. § 825.213(a)(2).

b. Paid Leave and the Recovery of Benefits

When an employee elects or an employer requires paid leave to be substituted for FMLA leave, the employer may not recover its share of group health benefits or other non-health benefit premiums for any period of FMLA leave covered by paid leave. 29 C.F.R. § 825.213(d). Because paid leave provided under a plan covering temporary disabilities, including workers' compensation, is not unpaid, recovery of health insurance premiums does not apply to these paid leaves.

c. Self–Insured Employers

The amount that self-insured employers may recover is limited to only the employer's share of allowable premiums as would be calculated under COBRA, excluding the two percent fee for administrative costs. 29 C.F.R. § 825.213(e).

d. Methods for Recovering the Employer's Benefit Payments

When an employee fails to return to work, any health and non-health benefit premiums which an employer is permitted to recover are a debt owed by the non-returning employee to the employer. 29 C.F.R. § 825.213(f). The existence of this debt does not alter the employer's responsibilities for group health benefit coverage and, under a self-insurance plan, payment of claims incurred during the FMLA leave.

To the extent recovery is permitted, the employer may recover the costs through deduction from any sums due to the employee (for example, unpaid wages, vacation pay, profit sharing, etc.), provided these deductions do not otherwise violate applicable federal or state wage payment or other laws. 29 C.F.R. § 825.213(f). To avoid these problems, the employer should have a written authorization from the employee permitting these deductions or an agreement to repay these monies. Alternatively, the employer may initiate legal action against the employee to recover these costs.

e. Employer's Recovery of Benefits Not Permitted Where an Employee Returns to Work

If the employee meets the return to work qualification period, the employer cannot recover its share of the group health plan benefits it paid. 29 C.F.R. § 825.213(c). The employee must return to work for at least thirty calendar days to prevent the employer's recovery of benefits it paid. After the employee satisfies the return to work period, recovery by the employer is prevented even though the employee is subsequently separated from employment by either the employer's or the employee's voluntary or involuntary action.

f. Employer's Recovery of Benefits Not Permitted Where an Employee Retires

An employee who retires is deemed to have returned to work for which the employer cannot recover its share of the group health benefits if the employee:

1. Transfers directly from taking FMLA leave to retirement or

2.   Retires during the first thirty days after the employee returns to work. 29 C.F.R. § 825.213(c).

H.   MORE GENEROUS BENEFITS

Nothing in the FMLA prevents an employer from providing more generous leave and benefit programs. However, they must comply with the FMLA during the FMLA leave's period. 29 U.S.C.A. § 2653; 29 C.F.R. § 825.700(b).

The FMLA's rights may not be diminished by any employment leave or benefit program. For example, a collective bargaining agreement which provides for reinstatement to a position that is not equivalent because of seniority or is at lesser pay, is superseded by the FMLA.

If an employer provides a longer unpaid family leave period than the FMLA, the employer is not required to extend additional FMLA rights, such as maintenance of group health benefits other than through COBRA, to the leave period not covered by the FMLA. 29 C.F.R. § 825.700(a).

I.   OUTSIDE EMPLOYMENT
WHILE ON LEAVE

If the employer has a uniformly-applied policy governing outside or supplemental employment, this policy may continue to apply to an employee on FMLA leave. 29 C.F.R. § 825.312(h). An employer who does not have this policy may not deny FMLA benefits an employee is entitled unless the FMLA leave was fraudulently obtained.

J. MEDICAL CERTIFICATION

An employer may require that an employee's leave be supported by a certification issued by the health care provider of the employee or the employee's ill family member:

1. To care for the employee's seriously-ill spouse, daughter, son, or parent or

2. Due to the employee's own serious health condition that makes the employee unable to perform one or more of the essential functions of the employee's position. 29 U.S.C.A. § 2613; 29 C.F.R. § 825.305(a).

An employer in its FMLA policy must give written notice that a medical certification may be required. 29 C.F.R. §§ 825.301, 825.305(a). An employer's oral request based on its written policy for a medical certification may be sufficient; however, a written request is better documentation should a dispute arise. 29 C.F.R. § 825.305(a).

When the leave is foreseeable and at least thirty days notice has been provided, the employee should provide the medical certification before the leave begins. 29 C.F.R. § 825.305(b). When this is not possible, the employee must provide the requested certification to the employer within the time frame requested by the employer. This time frame must allow at least fifteen calendar days after the employer's request, unless it is not practicable under the particular circumstances despite the employee's diligent, good faith efforts. 29 C.F.R. § 825.305(b).

At the time the employer requests certification, the employer must also advise an employee of the anticipated consequences of an employee's failure to provide adequate certification. 29 C.F.R. § 825.305(d). The employer must advise an employee whenever the employer finds a certification incomplete, and provide the employee a reasonable opportunity to cure any deficiency.

If the employer's sick or medical leave plan imposes medical certification requirements that are less stringent than the FMLA's certification requirements, and the employee or employer elects to substitute paid sick, vacation, personal, or family leave for unpaid FMLA leave where authorized, only the employer's less stringent sick leave certification requirements may be imposed. 29 C.F.R. § 825.305(e).

1. MEDICAL CERTIFICATION CONTENTS

a. Generally

The employee must provide a copy of a medical certification in a timely manner. 29 U.S.C.A. § 2613(a). A certification is generally sufficient if it states:

1. The date on which the serious health condition commenced;

2. The condition's probable duration; and

3. The appropriate medical facts within the health care provider's knowledge regarding the condition. 29 U.S.C.A. § 2613(b).

b. Medical Certification—Employee's Care of Spouse, Daughter, Son, or Parent with a Serious Health Condition

To care for a spouse, daughter, son, or parent of the employee, if this spouse, daughter, son, or parent has a serious health condition, the certification must include:

1. The date on which the serious health condition commenced;

2. The condition's probable duration;

3. The appropriate medical facts within the health care provider's knowledge regarding the condition;

4. A statement that the employee is needed to care for the spouse, daughter, son, or parent; and

5. An estimate of the amount of time that the employee is needed to care for the spouse, daughter, son, or parent. 29 U.S.C.A. § 2613(b)(4)(A), 29 C.F.R. § 825.306.

c. Medical Certification—Employee's Serious Health Condition

For a serious health condition that makes the employee unable to perform the functions of his or her position, the employee's certification must include:

1. The date on which the serious health condition commenced;

2. The condition's probable duration;

3. The appropriate medical facts within the health care provider's knowledge regarding the condition; and

4. A statement that the employee is unable to perform the functions of the position for which he or she is employed. 29 U.S.C.A. § 2613(b)(4)(B), 29 C.F.R. § 825.306.

d. Medical Certification—Intermittent Leave/ Reduced Leave Schedule—Employee's Care of Spouse, Daughter, Son, or Parent with a Serious Health Condition

To care for a spouse, daughter, son, or parent of the employee, if this spouse, daughter, son, or parent has a serious health condition, the certification for intermittent leave or leave on a reduced leave schedule must include a statement indicating:

1. That the employee is needed to care for the spouse, daughter, son, or parent who has a serious health condition or will assist in their recovery and

2. The intermittent leave's or reduced leave schedule's expected duration and schedule. 29 U.S.C.A. § 2613(b)(7), 29 C.F.R. § 825.306.

e. Medical Certification—Intermittent Leave/ Reduced Leave Schedule—Employee's Planned Medical Treatment

Where an employee takes intermittent leave or leave on a reduced leave schedule for planned medical treatment, the employee is required to provide a certification containing:

1. The dates on which the treatment is expected to be given and

2. The treatment's duration. 29 U.S.C.A. § 2613(b)(5), 29 C.F.R. § 825.306.

f. Medical Certification—Intermittent Leave/ Reduced Leave Schedule—Employee's Serious Health Condition

For a serious health condition that makes the employee unable to perform the functions of his or her position, the employee's certification for intermittent leave or leave on a reduced schedule must include a statement of:

1. The medical necessity for the leave and

2. The leave's expected duration. 29 U.S.C.A. § 2613(b)(6), 29 C.F.R. § 825.306.

g. Medical Certification—Second Opinion

An employer may require a second opinion from a second health care provider where the employer has reason to doubt the original certification's validity where the employee's FMLA leave is:

1. To care for the spouse, or a daughter, son, or parent of the employee, if this spouse, daugh-

ter, son, or parent has a serious health condition; or

2.   For a serious health condition that makes the employee unable to perform the functions of his or her position. 29 U.S.C.A. § 2613(c), 29 C.F.R. § 825.307(a)(2).

In securing the second opinion, the employer is entitled to information relating to:

1.   The date on which the serious health condition commenced;

2.   The condition's probable duration; and

3.   The appropriate medical facts within the health care provider's knowledge regarding the condition. 29 U.S.C.A. § 2613(c), 29 C.F.R. § 825.307(a)(2).

The employer must pay the employee's expense in securing the second opinion. 29 U.S.C.A. § 2613(c), 29 C.F.R. § 825.307(a)(2). However, the employer may designate the second health care provider or approve the employee's choice of the second health care provider. In neither case, can the health care provider who is engaged to provide the second opinion be employed on a regular basis by the employer. 29 U.S.C.A. § 2613(c)(2), 29 C.F.R. § 825.307(b).

Where the second opinion differs from the original certification's opinion, the employer may require, at the employer's expense, that the employee obtain a third health care provider's opinion. 29 U.S.C.A. § 2613(d), 29 C.F.R. § 825.307(c).

The third health care provider must be designated or approved jointly by the employee and the employer and must provide information regarding:

1.   The date on which the serious health condition commenced;

2.   The condition's probable duration; and

3.   The appropriate medical facts within the health care provider's knowledge regarding the condition. 29 U.S.C.A. § 2613(d), 29 C.F.R. § 825.307(c).

Where a third opinion is required, it shall be considered to be final and binding on the employee and the employer. 29 U.S.C.A. § 2613(d)(2), 29 C.F.R. § 825.307(c).

2.   MEDICAL CERTIFICATION FORM

The Department of Labor (DOL) has developed an optional form (Form WH–380, as revised) for employees' or their family members' use in obtaining medical certification, including second and third opinions, from health care providers that meets the FMLA's certification requirements. 29 C.F.R. § 825.306; see Chapter 6. This optional form reflects certification requirements to permit the health care provider to furnish appropriate medical information.

Form WH–380, as revised, or another form containing the same basic information, may be used by the employer; however, no additional information may be required. 29 C.F.R. § 825.306(b). In all instances, the information on the form must relate only to the serious health condition for which the current need for leave exists.

3. SUBSEQUENT RECERTIFICATIONS

The employer may require that the employee obtain subsequent recertifications on a reasonable basis. 29 U.S.C.A. § 2613(e); 29 C.F.R. § 825.308. For pregnancy, chronic, or permanent/long-term conditions under continuing supervision of a health care provider, an employer may request recertification no more often than every thirty days and only in connection with an absence by the employee, unless:

1. Circumstances described by the previous certification have changed significantly, for example, the duration or frequency of absences, the severity of the condition, complications, or

2. The employer receives information that casts doubt upon the employee's stated reason for the absence. 29 C.F.R. § 825.308(a).

If the minimum duration of the period of incapacity specified on a certification furnished by the health care provider is more than thirty days, the employer may not request recertification until that minimum duration has passed. 29 C.F.R. § 825.308(b)(1).

For FMLA leave taken intermittently or on a reduced leave schedule basis, the employer may not request recertification in less than the minimum period specified on the certification as necessary for this leave, including treatment. 29 C.F.R. § 825.308(b)(2).

An employer may request recertification at any reasonable interval, but not more often than every thirty days, unless:

1. The employee requests an extension of leave;

2. Circumstances described by the previous certification have changed significantly, for example, the duration of the illness, the nature of the illness, complications; or

3. The employer receives information that casts doubt upon the continuing validity of the certification. 29 C.F.R. § 825.308(c).

The employee must provide the requested recertification to the employer within the time frame requested by the employer which must allow at least fifteen calendar days after the employer's request, unless it is not practicable under the particular circumstances to do so despite the employee's diligent, good faith efforts. 29 C.F.R. § 825.308(d).

Any recertification requested by the employer is at the employee's expense unless the employer provides otherwise. 29 C.F.R. § 825.308(e). No second or third opinion on recertification may be required.

K. FRAUDULENT FMLA LEAVE

An employee who fraudulently obtains FMLA leave from an employer is not protected by the

FMLA's job restoration or maintenance of health benefits provisions. 29 C.F.R. § 825.312(g).

L. EMPLOYEE RESTORATION TO POSITION RIGHTS

1. GENERALLY

On return from FMLA leave, an employee is entitled to be returned to:

1. The same position the employee held when leave commenced or

2. An equivalent position with equivalent:

   i. Benefits;

   ii. Pay; and

   iii. Other terms and conditions of employment. 29 U.S.C.A. § 2614(a); 29 C.F.R. § 825.214(a).

An employee is entitled to this reinstatement even if:

1. The employee has been replaced or

2. His or her position has been restructured to accommodate the employee's absence. 29 C.F.R. § 825.214(a).

2. EMPLOYEE'S INABILITY TO PERFORM AN ESSENTIAL FUNCTION OF THE POSITION

If the employee is unable to perform an essential function of the position because of a physical or mental condition, including the continuation of a serious health condition, the employee has no right to restoration to another position under the FMLA. 29 C.F.R. § 825.214(b). However, the employer's obligations may still be governed by the Americans with Disabilities Act (ADA).

3. EQUIVALENT POSITION

An equivalent position is one that is virtually identical to the employee's former position in terms of:

1. Pay;

2. Benefits; and

3. Working conditions, including privileges, perquisites, and status. 29 U.S.C.A. § 2614(a)(1); 29 C.F.R. § 825.215(a).

The position must involve the same or substantially similar duties and responsibilities, which must entail substantially equivalent:

1. Skill;

2. Effort;

3. Responsibility; and

4. Authority. 29 C.F.R. § 825.215(a).

If an employee is no longer qualified for the position because of the employee's inability to attend a necessary course, renew a license, fly a minimum number of hours, etc., as a result of the leave, the employee must be given a reasonable opportunity to fulfill those conditions upon return to work. 29 C.F.R. § 825.215(b).

4. EQUIVALENT PAY

An employee is entitled to any unconditional pay increases that may have occurred during the FMLA leave period, for example, a cost of living increase. 29 C.F.R. § 825.215(c). Pay increases conditional upon seniority, length of service, or work performed need not be granted unless it is the employer's policy or practice to do so with respect to other employees on leave without pay. 29 C.F.R. § 825.215(c). In these cases, any pay increase would be granted based on the employee's seniority, length of service, work performed, etc., excluding the period of unpaid FMLA leave.

An employee is entitled to be restored to a position with the same or equivalent pay premiums, such as a shift differential. 29 C.F.R. § 825.215(c). If an employee departed from a position averaging ten hours of overtime and corresponding overtime pay each week, an employee is ordinarily entitled to the same type of a position on return from FMLA leave.

5. EQUIVALENT BENEFITS

a. Benefit Types

"Benefits" include all benefits provided or made available to employees by an employer, including:

1. Group life insurance;

2. Health insurance;

3. Disability insurance;

4. Sick leave;

5. Annual leave;

6. Educational benefits; and

7. Pensions. 29 C.F.R. § 825.215(d).

This is regardless of whether these benefits are provided by a practice or written policy of an employer through an employee benefit plan of the Employee Retirement Income Security Act (ERISA) of 1974. 29 U.S.C.A. § 1002(3). At the end of an employee's FMLA leave, benefits must be resumed in the same manner and at the same levels as provided when the leave began, and subject to any changes in benefit levels that may have taken place during the period of FMLA leave affecting the entire workforce, unless otherwise elected by the employee. 29 C.F.R. § 825.215(d)(1).

b. Changes in Benefit Plans While on Leave

Employees on unpaid FMLA leave are to be treated as if they continued to work for purposes of changes to benefit plans. 29 C.F.R. § 825.215(d)(5). They are entitled to changes in benefits plans, except those which may be dependent upon seniority or accrual during the leave period, immediately upon return from leave or to the same extent they would have qualified if no leave had been taken. 29 C.F.R. § 825.215(d)(5). For example, if the benefit plan is predicated on a pre-established number of hours worked each year and the employee does not have sufficient hours as a result of taking unpaid FMLA leave, the benefit is lost.

c. Requalifying for Benefits

Upon return from FMLA leave, an employee cannot be required to requalify for any benefits the employee enjoyed before the FMLA leave began, including family or dependent coverages. 29 C.F.R. § 825.215(d)(1). For example, if an employee was covered by a life insurance policy before taking leave but is not covered or coverage lapses during the period of unpaid FMLA leave, the employee cannot be required to meet any qualifications, such as taking a physical examination, to requalify for life insurance upon return from leave. This may require some employers to modify life insurance and other benefits programs to restore employees to equivalent benefits upon return from FMLA leave by:

1. Making arrangements for continued payment of costs to maintain these benefits during the unpaid FMLA leave or

2. Paying these costs subject to recovery from the employee on return from leave. 29 C.F.R. §§ 825.213(b), 825.215(d)(1).

d. Accrual of Benefits While on Leave

An employee may, but is not entitled to, accrue any additional benefits or seniority during an unpaid FMLA leave. 29 C.F.R. § 825.215(d)(2). Benefits accrued at the time leave began, however, for example, paid vacation, sick or personal leave to the extent not substituted for FMLA leave, must be available to an employee upon return from leave.

e. Continuation of Benefits for Which the Employee Typically Pays

If, while on unpaid FMLA leave, an employee desires to continue life insurance, disability insurance, or other types of benefits for which he or she typically pays, the employer is required to follow established policies or practices for continuing these benefits for other instances of leave without pay. 29 C.F.R. § 825.215(d)(3). If the employer has no established policy, the employee and the employer should agree upon arrangements before the FMLA leave begins.

f. Pension and Retirement Plans

With respect to pension and other retirement plans, any period of unpaid FMLA leave cannot be treated as or counted toward a break in service for purposes of:

1. Vesting and

2. Eligibility to participate. 29 C.F.R. § 825.215(d)(4).

Also, if the plan requires an employee to be employed on a specific date to be credited with a year of service for vesting, contributions, or participation purposes, an employee on unpaid FMLA leave on that date must be deemed to have been employed on that date. 29 C.F.R. § 825.215(d) (4). However, unpaid FMLA leave periods need not be treated as credited service for purposes of:

1. Benefit accrual;
2. Vesting; and
3. Eligibility to participate. 29 C.F.R. § 825.215(d) (4).

g. Bonuses

Many employers pay bonuses in different forms to employees for job-related performance. These may include bonuses for:

1. Perfect attendance;
2. Safety (absence of injuries or accidents on the job); and
3. Exceeding production goals. 29 C.F.R. § 825.215(c)(2).

Bonuses for perfect attendance and safety do not require performance by the employee but rather contemplate the absence of occurrences. To the extent an employee who takes FMLA leave has met all the requirements for either or both of these bonuses before FMLA leave began, the employee is entitled to continue this entitlement upon return from FMLA leave; i.e, the employee may not be disqualified for the bonuses for the taking of FMLA leave. 29 C.F.R. § 825.215(c)(2).

A monthly production bonus, however, does require the employee's performance. If the employee is on FMLA leave during any part of the period for which this bonus is computed, the employee is entitled to the same consideration for the bonus as other employees on paid or unpaid leave as appropriate. 29 C.F.R. § 825.215(c)(2).

2. EQUIVALENT TERMS AND CONDITIONS OF EMPLOYMENT

a. Generally

An equivalent position must have substantially similar duties, conditions, responsibilities, privileges and status as the employee's original position. 29 C.F.R. § 825.215(e). The employee must have the same or an equivalent opportunity for:

1. Bonuses;

2. Profit-sharing; and

3. Other similar discretionary and non-discretionary payments. 29 C.F.R. § 825.215(e).

The requirement that an employee be restored to the same or equivalent job with the same or equivalent pay, benefits, and terms and conditions of employment does not extend to de minimis or intangible, unmeasurable aspects of the job. 29 C.F.R. § 825.215(f).

b. Worksite Location

The employee must be reinstated to the same or a geographically approximate worksite. 29 C.F.R. § 825.215(e)(1). This involves a worksite that does not require a significant increase in commuting time or distance from where the employee had previously been employed.

c. Worksite Closure

If the employee's original worksite has been closed, the employee is entitled to the same rights as if the employee had not been on leave when the worksite closed. 29 C.F.R. § 825.215(e)(1). For example, if an employer transfers all employees from a closed worksite to a new worksite in a different city, the employee on leave is also entitled to transfer under the same conditions as if he or she had continued to be employed.

d. Shift and Schedule

The employee is ordinarily entitled to return to the:

1. Same shift or

2. The same or an equivalent work schedule. 29 C.F.R. § 825.215(e)(2)

The FMLA does not prohibit an employer from accommodating an employee's request to be restored to a different shift, schedule, or position which better suits the employee's personal needs on return from leave, or to offer a promotion to a better position. 29 C.F.R. § 825.215(e)(4). However, an employee cannot be induced by the employer to accept a different position against the employee's wishes. 29 C.F.R. § 825.215(e)(4).

3. LIMITATIONS ON AN EMPLOYER'S OBLIGATION TO REINSTATE

An employee has no greater right to reinstatement or to other benefits and conditions of employment than if the employee had been continuously employed during the FMLA leave. 29 C.F.R. § 825.216(a). An employer must be able to show that an employee would not otherwise have been employed at the time reinstatement is requested to deny restoration. Reinstatement is not required for:

1. *Layoff.* If an employee is laid off during the FMLA leave and employment is terminated, the employer's responsibility to continue FMLA leave, maintain group health plan benefits, and restore the employee cease at the time the employee is laid off, provided the employer has no continuing obligations under a collective bargaining agreement or otherwise.

2. *Shift Elimination.* If a shift has been eliminated, or overtime has been decreased, an employee would not be entitled to return to work that shift or the original overtime hours upon restoration.

3. *Specific Term Employment.* If an employee was hired for a specific term or only to perform work on a definite project, the employer has no obligation to restore the employee if the employment term or project is over; however, if an employee was hired to perform

work on a contract, and after that contract period the contract was awarded to another contractor, the successor contractor may be required to restore the employee if it is a successor employer.

4. *Key Employee.* An employer may deny job restoration to salaried eligible employees or "key employees" if this denial is necessary to prevent substantial and grievous economic injury to the operations of the employer, or may delay restoration to an employee who fails to provide a fitness for duty certificate to return to work.

5. *Workers' Compensation.* If the employee has been on a workers' compensation absence during which FMLA leave has been taken concurrently, and after twelve weeks of FMLA leave the employee is unable to return to work, the employee no longer has the protections of the FMLA and must look to the workers' compensation statute or Americans with Disabilities Act (ADA) for any relief or protections. 29 C.F.R. § 825.216.

CHAPTER 5

LITIGATION UNDER THE FAMILY AND MEDICAL LEAVE ACT (FMLA)

A. INTRODUCTION

Because of its complexities, the Family and Medical Leave Act (FMLA) of 1993 and the Department of Labor's (DOL's) implementing regulations have generated considerable litigation over eligibility, notice, reinstatement, retaliation, and serious health conditions. Pub. L. No. 103–3, 107 Stat. 6 (1993); *codified at* 2 U.S.C.A. §§ 1301, 1302, 1312, 1381–1385, 1401–1416; 5 U.S.C.A. §§ 6381–6387; 29 U.S.C.A. §§ 2601, 2611–2619, 2631–2636, 2651–2654; 29 C.F.R. §§ 825.100–825.800. This chapter reviews the court decisions interpreting the FMLA and its regulations.

B. THE FEDERAL FAMILY AND MEDICAL LEAVE ACT'S (FMLA'S) ENFORCEMENT SINCE 1993

In 1997, the Department of Labor (DOL) released a report discussing the Family and Medical Leave Act's (FMLA's) enforcement since 1993. DEPARTMENT OF LABOR, 41 MONTHS OF ENFORCEMENT AND OUTREACH ACTIVITY (AUGUST 5,

1993—DECEMBER 31, 1996) (1997) [hereinafter 1997 REPORT]. A follow-up report was released by the DOL in August 1998 providing additional statistics and conclusions. DEPARTMENT OF LABOR, FIVE YEARS OF SUCCESS (AUGUST 5, 1993—AUGUST 5, 1998) (1998) [hereinafter 1998 REPORT]. These reports are important to gain a better understanding of the FMLA's enforcement and litigation trends.

According to the 1998 Report, 12,633 complaints were received and ninety percent were successfully resolved. 1998 REPORT. The 1997 Report indicated that 8,358 complaints were received and compliance actions were completed on 7,433 complaints. 1997 REPORT. In one year, the complaint number increased by thirty-three percent illustrating the FMLA's litigation potential.

Fifty-nine percent of the 1997 Report's complaints were found to be valid. 1997 REPORT. Forty-one percent of the complaints were not covered by or were found not to violate the FMLA. 1997 REPORT.

The 1997 Report indicated that the valid complaints involved:

1. *Employee Reinstatement.* Forty percent concerned an employer's refusal to reinstate an employee to the same or equivalent position;

2. *Leave Granting.* Twenty-three percent dealt with an employer's refusal to grant an FMLA leave;

3. *Interference with Employee Rights.* Ten percent were related to an employer's interference with or discrimination against an employee using an FMLA leave;

4. *Benefit Continuation.* Four percent alleged that an employer refused to maintain an employee's group health plan benefits;

5. *Multiple Reasons.* Fourteen percent; and

6. *Other Reasons.* Nine percent.

The 1998 Report did not note any significant changes from the 1997 Report regarding employee complaint areas. 1998 REPORT. However, in the 1998 Report, forty-five per-cent of the employees alleged their employers refused to reinstate them after an FMLA leave while twenty-two percent complained that they were refused FMLA leave. 1998 REPORT.

With the 1997 Report and the 1998 Report in mind, the following areas have resulted in FMLA court interpretations:

1.   ABSENTEEISM

An employer has the right to demand that employees regularly attend work. On occasion, employees may be absent from work for illness, a family member's sickness, or another reason. When this occurs, an employer can voluntarily permit these absences, be required to grant them under a collective bargaining agreement, or be mandated to provide them under a federal or state statute. These absences may be paid or unpaid.

Employee absences that are required to be granted under a federal or state statute are protected. For example, FMLA leave is statutorily protected. 29 U.S.C.A. § 2654; 29 C.F.R. §§ 825.100–825.800.

FMLA leave is not unlimited. Where FMLA leave is exhausted or where employer procedures for requesting, continuing, or returning from the leave are not complied with, the employee may be subject to discipline up to and including termination for absenteeism.

The employer may not violate the FMLA's retaliation provision when it terminates an employee for absenteeism. 29 U.S.C.A. § 2615(a); 29 C.F.R. § 825.220. The employer's evidence must show that the employee was terminated for absenteeism, and not because of a request for or due to an FMLA leave. This is a heavy employer burden of proof. See *Hypes v. First Commerce Corporation*, 134 F.3d 721 (5th Cir.1998); *Oswalt v. Sara Lee Corporation*, 889 F.Supp. 253 (N.D.Miss., 1995), *aff'd*, 74 F.3d 91 (5th Cir.1996); *Bauer v. Dayton–Walther Corp.*, 910 F.Supp. 306 (E.D.Ky.1996), *aff'd*, 118 F.3d 1109 (6th Cir.1997); *Stoops v. One Call Communications*, 141 F.3d 309 (7th Cir.1998); *Holmes v. Boeing Company*, 166 F.3d 1221 (10th Cir.1999).

2. AFTER–ACQUIRED EVIDENCE

The after-acquired evidence doctrine as applied to employment law is a fairly recent legal development. Its application to employment law first arose in discrimination cases during the 1980s. See *Smallwood v. United Air Lines, Inc.*, 728 F.2d 614, 627 (4th Cir.1984), *cert. denied*, 469 U.S. 832 (1984); see also *McKennon v. Nashville Banner Publishing Co.*, 513 U.S. 352 (1995).

An FMLA case that would involve the doctrine would proceed as follows: The employer terminates an employee for an alleged illegal reason under the FMLA. The employee then files an FMLA claim against the employer. Before trial, the employer uncovers some type of employee wrongdoing that would have been grounds for termination had the employer known of the wrongdoing before the actual termination. The wrongdoing could have occurred either while the employee was employed or before the employee was hired, for example, a misrepresentation on a resume. At trial, the employer offers evidence of the wrongdoing as a defense to the discrimination claim against it.

The arguments that support the after-acquired evidence doctrine have been based on a variety of legal theories. These applications depend upon the particular factual situation. The justification arguments include fraud in the inducement, unclean hands, lack of injury, comparative negligence, and mixed-motive analysis. See generally *McKennon v. Nashville Banner Publishing Co.*, 513 U.S. 352 (1995).

The after-acquired evidence doctrine has been applied in FMLA litigation. For example, factual issues precluded a summary judgment on a college's claim that an assistant dean was not entitled to back wages. *Hillman v. Hamilton College*, 1998 WL 166827, 4 Wage & Hour Cas.2d (BNA) 1035 (N.D.N.Y.1998). The college's assistant dean, whose contract was not renewed after she took an FMLA leave, may have acted inappropriately in copying documents from her personnel file. Had it known of her actions, the college would have terminated her.

3. AMERICANS WITH DISABILITIES ACT (ADA)/FAMILY MEDICAL LEAVE ACT (FMLA)

The FMLA does not modify or preempt the Americans with Disabilities Act (ADA). 29 U.S.C.A. § 2651(a); 29 C.F.R. § 825.702(a). The FMLA's leave provisions are wholly distinct from the ADA's reasonable accommodation obligations for employers. An employer must provide leave under whichever FMLA or ADA statutory provision provides the employee greater rights. However, when the FMLA's and ADA's remedies coincide, the employee may only utilize one statute's relief. See *Laffey v. Northwest Airlines, Inc.*, 567 F.2d 429, 445 (D.C.Cir. 1976), *cert. denied*, 434 U.S. 1086 (1978).

An employee with a history of back injuries had no FMLA claim arising from the employer's requirement that he undergo a functional capacity examination to determine if he was physically able to return to work. *Porter v. United States Alumoweld Company*, 125 F.3d 243 (4th Cir.1997). Even though the FMLA's regulations provide that a fitness for duty certification under the FMLA need only be a simple statement of the employee's ability to return to work, the employer had grounds under the Americans with Disabilities Act (ADA) to request the examination. The FMLA implies that an employee may be required to meet the fitness requirements of both statutes.

4. CARE FOR A RELATIVE

The FMLA permits an employee to take FMLA leave for the care of a spouse, daughter, son, or parent of the employee with a serious health condition. 29 U.S.C.A. § 2612(a)(1)(C); 29 C.F.R. § 825.112(a)(3). An employee's daughter's upper respiratory infection was a "serious health condition" which satisfied the FMLA's requirements. *Brannon v. OshKosh B'Gosh, Inc.*, 897 F.Supp. 1028 (M.D.Tenn.1995); see also *Barron v. Runyon*, 11 F.Supp.2d 676 (E.D.Va.1998) (care of wife).

An employee's child, however, who was suspected of being sexually molested did not have a serious health condition under the FMLA. *Martyszenko v. Safeway*, 120 F.3d 120 (8th Cir.1997). Likewise, FMLA leave to take care of a deceased relative was denied. *Brown v. J.C. Penney Corp.*, 924 F.Supp. 1158 (S.D.Fla.1996); see also *Sakellarion v. Judge & Dolph, Ltd.*, 893 F.Supp. 800 (N.D.Ill.1995) (daughter's asthma attack over the weekend not considered a serious health condition); *Seidle v. Provident Mutual Life Ins. Co.*, 871 F.Supp. 238

(E.D.Pa.1994) (child's ear infection (otitis media) was not a serious health condition within the meaning of the FMLA).

An employer was not required to give an employee FMLA leave after her son's death. *Beal v. Rubbermaid Commercial Products*, 972 F.Supp. 1216 (S.D.Iowa 1997). FMLA leave was not meant for bereavement.

5.   CHILD LEAVE—BIRTH/PLACEMENT

The FMLA permits an employee to take FMLA leave for the birth of an employee's daughter or son and for the placement of a daughter or son with the employee for adoption or foster care. 29 U.S.C.A. §§ 2612(a)(1)(A);   2612(a)(1)(B);   29   C.F.R. §§ 825.112(a)–825.112(c). Summary judgment was inappropriate on an employee's claim that an employer discriminated against her for attempting to exercise her right to pregnancy leave benefits under the FMLA when the employer terminated her one day before she was to begin leave. *Dumoulin v. Formica*, 968 F.Supp. 68 (N.D.N.Y.1997). Likewise, an FMLA claim was stated for denying an employee leave following a daughter's birth. *Knussman v. State of Maryland*, 935 F.Supp. 659 (D.Md.1996).

An employee who alleged that he took leave to travel to New York to place a young girl in his custody for adoption or foster care stated an FMLA claim, even if he was the young girl's biological father. *Kelley v. Crosfield Catalysts*, 135 F.3d 1202 (7th Cir.1998). FMLA leave for adoption or foster care expires twelve months from the placement date. *Bocalbos v. National Western Life Insurance*, 162 F.3d 379 (5th Cir.1998) (FMLA leave to bring two children employee adopted three years earlier to the United States properly denied).

6. COLLECTIVE BARGAINING AGREEMENTS AND THE FMLA

Collective bargaining agreements may effect FMLA leave. Immediately after the FMLA's adoption this arose over the FMLA's effective date for collective bargaining agreements. 29 U.S.C.A. § 2601 note; 29 C.F.R. §§ 825.102, 825.103, 825.700(c). An employee who was on leave between February 1993 and February 1994 was not found eligible for FMLA leave. *Caruthers v. Proctor & Gamble*, 961 F.Supp. 1484 (D.Kan.1997). The FMLA first became effective for employees covered by collective bargaining agreements on February 5, 1994. The employee's time spent on leave did not count towards the required hours of service.

The FMLA's leave procedures may be covered in a collective bargaining agreement's provisions. 29 C.F.R. § 825.700(c). An employer properly sent a notice pursuant to a collective bargaining agreement requiring an employee on FMLA leave to undergo a second opinion medical examination to the employee's last address of record. *Diaz v. Fort Wayne Foundry Corporation*, 131 F.3d 711 (7th Cir.1997).

7. CONTINUING TREATMENT

"Continuing treatment" requires that the employee be incapacitated to qualify for an FMLA leave. 29 C.F.R. § 825.800. Under the FMLA's regulations, it also includes examinations to determine if a serious health condition exists and evaluations of a condition as treatment. *Stubl v. T. A. Systems, Inc.*, 984 F.Supp. 1075 (E.D.Mich.1997).

Migraine headaches have qualified as continuing treatment. *Vargo-Adams v. United States Postal Service*, 992 F.Supp. 939 (N.D.Ohio 1998); *Hendry v. GTE North, Inc.*, 896 F.Supp. 816 (N.D.Ind.1995). A peptic ulcer's flare-up may qualify. *Victorelli v. Shadyside Hospital*, 128 F.3d 184 (3d Cir.1997). Treatment of Ikeloids may also qualify. *Sheppard v. Diversified Foods and Seasonings, Inc.*, 1996 WL 54440, 5 A.D. Cas. (BNA) 479 (E.D.La.1996).

Continuing treatment, however, was not found where an employer terminated an employee who suffered from hypertension and atrial fibrillation. *Hodgens v. General Dynamics*, 963 F.Supp. 102 (D.R.I.), *aff'd*, 144 F.3d 151 (1st Cir.1998). The employee's condition did not prevent him from performing his job. His doctor did not recommend that he stay out of work. He saw the doctor for periodic checkups without missing work time.

8. DAMAGES

The FMLA permits damages to be recovered for violations.   29   U.S.C.A.   § 2617;   29   C.F.R. § 825.400(c). Damages are calculated as follows:

a. Attorneys' Fees

The FMLA permits the recovery of attorneys' fees. 29 U.S.C.A. § 2617(a)(3).

i. *Standard for Determining*

The FMLA attorneys' fee provision requires a court to award some meaningful measure of attorneys' fees. 29 U.S.C.A. § 2617(a)(3). The factors enunciated in *Johnson v. Georgia Highway Express, Inc.*, 488 F.2d 714 (5 Cir.1974), are used as a guide for determining the attorneys' fees reasonableness. *McDonnell v. Miller Oil Co.*, 968 F.Supp. 288 (E.D.Va.1997), *aff'd without op.*, 110 F.3d 60 (4th Cir.1997), *remanded*, 134 F.3d 638 (4th Cir.1998).

ii. *Employees' Attorneys' Fees*

The FMLA permits a successful employee to recover reasonable attorneys' fees. 29 U.S.C.A. § 2617(a)(3). A court was required to award some meaningful measure of attorneys' fees to an employee whom a jury awarded only $2.00 in damages. *McDonnell v. Miller Oil Co.*, 968 F.Supp. 288 (E.D.Va.1997), *aff'd*, 110 F.3d 60 (4th Cir.1997), *remanded*, 134 F.3d 638 (4th Cir.1998). The employee was entitled to $19,698.81 for FMLA attorneys' fees.

iii. *Employer's Attorneys' Fees*

Even though the FMLA does not permit an employer to recover attorneys' fees, a successful employer may attempt to recover these fees under the Equal Access to Justice Act. 29 U.S.C.A. § 2617(a)(3). An employer that prevailed in a Department of Labor's (DOL's) FMLA action attempted to recover attorneys' fees against the DOL. *Reich v. Midwest Plastic Engineering*, 934 F.Supp. 266 (W.D.Mich.1996), *aff'd without op.*, 113 F.3d 1235 (6th Cir.1997). The employer, however, was not entitled to attorneys' fees under the Equal Access to Justice Act because the DOL's position was substantially justified.

b. Backpay

The FMLA permits backpay to be awarded. 29 U.S.C.A. § 2617(a)(1)(A)(i)(I). Backpay, however, cannot be awarded to an employee for the period of the FMLA leave where the leave is unpaid. *Barrilleaux v. Thayer Lodging Group*, 1998 WL 411385, 4 Wage & Hour Cas.2d (BNA) 1472 (E.D.La.1998).

c. Front Pay

The FMLA permits front pay to be awarded. 29 U.S.C.A. § 2617(a)(1)(B). Front pay, as an alternative or complement to reinstatement, is an equitable remedy best determined by the court and not a jury. *Cline v. Wal–Mart Stores*, 144 F.3d 294 (4th Cir.1998).

d. Benefits

Lost benefits may be recovered under the FMLA. 29 U.S.C.A. § 2617(a)(1)(A)(i)(II). Employees who were not informed about the availability of FMLA leave before, during, or after their medical leaves were entitled to reimbursement for the employer's portion of their health insurance that they paid while on leave for a period of twelve weeks. *Herman v. Princeton City Schools*, 1997 WL 861836, 4 Wage & Hour Cas.2d (BNA) 702 (S.D. Ohio 1997).

e. Loss of Job Security

Loss of job security, assuming there is a legal or contractual right to it, is a subject of FMLA damages. 29 U.S.C.A. § 2617(a)(1)(A)(i)(II); see *Lloyd v. Wyoming Valley Health Care*, 994 F.Supp. 288 (M.D.Pa.1998).

f. Child Care and Parental Care Costs

An employee may recover child care and parental care costs. 29 U.S.C.A. § 2617(a)(1)(A)(i)(II); see *Barrilleaux v. Thayer Lodging Group*, 1998 WL 614181, 4 Wage & Hour Cas.2d (BNA) 1725 (E.D.La.1998).

g. Costs

Costs are recoverable under the FMLA. 29 U.S.C.A. § 2617(a)(3); see *McDonnell v. Miller Oil Co.*, 968 F.Supp. 288 (E.D.Va.1997), *aff'd*, 110 F.3d 60 (4th Cir.1997), *remanded*, 134 F.3d 638 (4th Cir.1998).

h. Emotional Distress

An employee bringing an FMLA action may not seek punitive damages and recovery for pain and suffering, anxiety, humiliation, physical injury, and emotional distress. See *Godwin v. Rheem Manufacturing Co.*, 15 F. Supp.2d 1197 (M.D.Ala.1998); *Lloyd v. Wyoming Valley Health Care*, 994 F.Supp. 288 (M.D.Pa.1998); *Settle v. S.W. Rodgers Company*, 998 F.Supp. 657 (E.D.Va.1998).

i. Liquidated Damages

Liquidated damages are recoverable under the FMLA. 29 U.S.C.A. § 2617(a)(1)(A)(iii); see *Herman v. Princeton City Schools*, 1997 WL 861836, 4 Wage & Hour Cas.2d (BNA) 702 (S.D. Ohio 1997); *Dintino v. Doubletree Hotels*, 1997 WL 717208, 4 Wage & Hour Cas.2d (BNA) 413 (E.D.Pa.1997); *Morris v. VCW, Inc.*, 1996 WL 740544, 3 Wage & Hour Cas.2d (BNA) 1272 (W.D.Mo.1996).

j. Punitive Damages

Courts are not unanimous over whether punitive damages can be recovered under the FMLA. For example, some courts have indicated that an employee bringing an FMLA action may not seek punitive damages and recovery for pain and suffering, anxiety, humiliation, physical injury, and emotional distress. See *Godwin v. Rheem Manufacturing Co.*, 15 F. Supp.2d 1197 (M.D.Ala.1998); *Settle v. S.W. Rodgers Company*, 998 F.Supp. 657 (E.D.Va.1998).

Where an employer, however, sought to dismiss damage claims for punitive damages and mental distress damages, the court dismissed the employer's claims. *McAnnally v. Wyn South Molded Products, Inc.*, 912 F.Supp. 512 (N.D.Ala.1996). It found that the FMLA's language was clear concerning "other compensation" as a measurement of damages. The terms wages, salary, and employment benefits implied a "quid pro quo" exchange between an employer and its employee.

k. Reinstatement Offer

An employee who alleged that she was denied an FMLA leave would not be entitled to any backpay after the date on which the employer made an unconditional reinstatement offer. *Barrilleaux v. Thayer Lodging Group*, 1998 WL 411385, 4 Wage & Hour Cas.2d (BNA) 1472 (E.D.La.1998). However, the employee could still recover damages prior to the employer's unconditional reinstatement offer. *Barrilleaux v. Thayer Lodging Group*, 1998 WL 614181, 4 Wage & Hour Cas.2d (BNA) 1725 (E.D.La.1998).

l. Withholding Taxes

An employer improperly withheld federal and state income taxes and FICA contributions from an FMLA judgment owed to an employee although federal law required withholding of taxes and FICA from wages. *Churchill v. Star Enterprises*, 3 F. Supp.2d 622 (E.D.Pa.1998). The jury's award did not represent wages for services performed. The employer could not withhold taxes on account of employee benefits. The jury's award did not delineate between wages and benefits.

9. DISABILITY FRAUD

An employer may terminate an employee who commits disability fraud while on FMLA leave. 29 C.F.R. § 825.312(g); see *Kariotis v. Navistar International Transportation*, 131 F.3d 672 (7th Cir. 1997).

10. DISCRIMINATION

An employer cannot discriminate against an employee for requesting or taking an FMLA leave. 29 U.S.C.A. § 2615(a)(2); 29 C.F.R. § 825.220(c). Summary judgment was inappropriate on an employee's claim that an employer discriminated against her for attempting to exercise her right to pregnancy leave benefits under the FMLA when the employer terminated her one day before she was to begin the leave. *Dumoulin v. Formica*, 968 F.Supp. 68 (N.D.N.Y.1997).

A restaurant, however, did not violate the FMLA when it demoted a dining room supervisor while she was on FMLA leave. *Dollar v. Shoney's, Inc.*, 981 F.Supp. 1417 (N.D.Ala.1997). The supervisor failed to show that the restaurant's legitimate nondiscriminatory reasons for the demotion, namely her inadequate work performance and need for supervisory changes to improve product quality and customer satisfaction, were pretextual.

11. EMPLOYEE ELIGIBILITY

To qualify for an FMLA leave, the employee must have been employed for at least twelve months by his/her employer and for at least 1,250 hours with his/her employer during the previous twelve months. 29 U.S.C.A. § 2611(2)(A); 29 C.F.R. §§ 825.110, 825.111. Employee eligibility may arise regarding:

a. Hours/Months Worked

The FMLA requires that the employee must have been employed for at least 1,250 hours with his/her employer during the previous twelve months. 29 U.S.C.A. § 2611(2)(A); 29 C.F.R. §§ 825.110, 825.111. An employee is not eligible for an FMLA leave who works less than the required 1,250 hours. *Rockwell v. Mack Trucks*, 8 F. Supp.2d 499 (D.Md. 1998); see also *Caruthers v. Proctor & Gamble*, 961 F.Supp. 1484 (D.Kan.1997); *Seaman v. Downtown Partnership*, 991 F.Supp. 751 (D.Md.1998); *Mion v. Aftermarket Tool & Equipment*, 990 F.Supp. 535 (W.D.Mich.1997).

Hours worked with distinct and separate employer entities cannot be combined to establish FMLA leave eligibility. *Rollins v. Wilson County Government*, 967 F.Supp. 990 (M.D.Tenn.1997). An employee's work with a predecessor company, however, may be used to establish hours worked for FMLA eligibility. For example, an employee who was employed by the employer's predecessor was permitted to show that the hours worked with the former employer should be credited for FMLA leave eligibility. *Lange v. Showbiz Pizza Time*, 12 F. Supp.2d 1150 (D.Kan.1998).

Vacation days, personal holidays, days of suspension, holidays, and sick days are not counted as "hours of service" in determining employee eligibility. The FMLA requires that hours of service must be determined by applying the Fair Labor Standards Act's (FLSA's) principles. 29 C.F.R. Part 785. Neither paid leave or unpaid leave is hours worked under the FLSA. *Clark v. Allegheny University Hospital*, 1998 WL 94803, 4 Wage & Hour Cas.2d (BNA) 744 (E.D.Pa.1998).

To deny an FMLA leave, the employer must maintain adequate records to verify that the required hours were not worked by the employee. 29 C.F.R. § 825.500. An airline employer, however, that failed to keep records of time that a flight attendant spent working after the flight "blocked in" was still able to establish that the attendant was not an FMLA eligible employee. *Robinson-Scott v. Delta Airlines*, 4 F. Supp.2d 1183 (N.D.Ga.1998). It determined how much time the attendant spent working after the flight "blocked in" by multiplying the time she remained on board after the "block in" by the number of duty periods. This formula established that the attendant did not work the required 1,250 hours. See also *Cantrell v. Delta Airlines*, 2 F. Supp.2d 1460 (N.D.Ga.1998); *Rich v. Delta Air Lines, Inc.*, 921 F.Supp. 767 (N.D.Ga.1996).

b. Intermittent Leave

An employee who is eligible for intermittent FMLA leave need only establish eligibility on occasion for the first absence and not for each subsequent absence. *Barron v. Runyon*, 11 F. Supp.2d 676 (E.D.Va.1998).

c. Temporary Employees

A temporary employee may qualify for FMLA leave. For example, an employee who was assigned by a temporary employment agency to a company's facility in December 1994, became a permanent employee of the company in July 1995. *Miller v. Defiance Metal Products*, 989 F.Supp. 945 (N.D.Ohio 1997). The employee worked at the company's facility for the twelve month period. Her reclassification from a temporary employee to a permanent employee did not alter the time period for calculating FMLA eligibility.

d. Laid–Off Employees

The term "employee" for FMLA purposes includes laid-off employees. 29 C.F.R. § 825.216(A)(1); see *Duckworth v. Pratt & Whitney, Inc.*, 152 F.3d 1 (1st Cir.1998). An employee who is laid off, however, cannot take an FMLA leave that is not eligible for the leave. *Brohm v. JH Properties*, 149 F.3d 517 (6th Cir.1998).

e. Employee Resignations

Resigning from employment prior to requesting an FMLA leave does not entitle an employee to an

FMLA leave. *Hammon v. DHL Airways*, 165 F.3d 441 (6th Cir.1999). Also, a resignation does not entitle an employee to be restored to the same or equivalent position upon completing the FMLA leave. *Walthall v. Fulton County School District*, 18 F. Supp.2d 1378 (N.D.Ga.1998).

12. EMPLOYEE NOTICE

Generally, an employee must provide the employer with thirty days advance notice for a foreseeable FMLA leave. Where this notice is not possible, notice must be given as soon as practicable. 29 U.S.C.A. § 2612(e); 29 C.F.R. §§ 825.302, 825.303.

a. Adequate Notice

Employees who take time off do not have to expressly mention the FMLA when they notify their employers of their need for leave. *Manuel v. Westlake Polymers Corp.*, 66 F.3d 758 (5th Cir.1995). The FMLA's notice provision, which requires employees to notify their employers of their need to take FMLA leave, does not require employees to mention the FMLA by name. Congress, in enacting the FMLA, did not intend to impose this onerous requirement on employees. Employees simply need to state that a leave is needed. It then becomes the employer's obligation to inquire whether or not the employee is requesting FMLA leave.

Verbal notice may be sufficient. An employee's verbal notice that he would be absent because of a headache may be adequate FMLA notice. *Ware v.*

Stahl Specialty Company, 1998 WL 184267, 4 Wage & Hour Cas.2d (BNA) 974 (W.D.Mo.1998). The employee informed his employer when he began employment that he took prescription medication for migraine headaches. His supervisors were aware that he took a number of days off because of migraine attacks. The employee had also submitted doctor's notes that the absence was due to migraine headaches.

An employee provided sufficient verbal notice that she was requesting FMLA leave at the time of her last absence. *Hendry v. GTE North, Inc.*, 896 F.Supp. 816 (N.D.Ind.1995). The migraines were a serious health condition. Also, an employee's failure to inform her employer that she was taking FMLA leave did not affect her being protected by the FMLA so long as she gave some form of notice of her daughter's serious health condition. *Peters v. Community Action Committee*, 977 F.Supp. 1428 (M.D.Ala.1997).

Written notification is sufficient to put the employer on notice. Summary judgment was inappropriate where the employee testified that she completed a written notification and specifically stated that her absences were due to headaches. *Vargo-Adams v. United States Postal Service*, 992 F.Supp. 939 (N.D.Ohio 1998). An employee's conduct in filling out a city-provided leave request form, indicating that the cause was medical need, and attaching a doctor's note requiring her to take time off was sufficient to put the city on notice that this was a possible FMLA leave. *Price v. Fort Wayne*, 117

F.3d 1022 (7th Cir.1997); see also *Brannon v. Osh-Kosh B'Gosh, Inc.*, 897 F.Supp. 1028 (M.D.Tenn. 1995) (employee gave sufficient notice of her daughter's serious health condition through a doctor's note).

b. Inadequate Notice

An employee must give an employer reasonable notice to determine that an FMLA leave situation exists. Inadequate notice existed where an employee's wife/coworker called the employer on the first day of the employee's absence and said that she and her husband would be out for awhile. *Carter v. Ford Motor Company*, 121 F.3d 1146 (8th Cir.1997). The employee also informed the labor relations officer five days later that he would be out and did not know when he would return. No further information was provided.

Employees cannot withhold information regarding an absence. *Gay v. Gilman Paper Company*, 125 F.3d 1432 (11th Cir.1997). The employer can require an employee on FMLA leave to report periodically regarding his/her status. *Reich v. Midwest Plastic Engineering*, 934 F.Supp. 266 (W.D.Mich. 1996), *aff'd without op.*, 113 F.3d 1235 (6th Cir. 1997).

Employees cannot claim ignorance of the FMLA's requirements where the employer has complied with the FMLA's posting requirements. An employee could not justify his failure to follow the FMLA's procedure for giving notice by claiming that he never knew of the FMLA. *Kaylor v. Fannin Region-*

al Hospital, 946 F.Supp. 988 (N.D.Ga.1996). The employer satisfied the FMLA's notice requirements by posting the FMLA notice in employee break rooms and discussing the FMLA in the employee handbook and in employee risk management sessions. The employee also received FMLA information during a previous FMLA leave.

13.   EMPLOYER COVERAGE

An employer must employ a sufficient number of employees to fall within the FMLA's coverage. 29 U.S.C.A. § 2611(4)(A); 29 C.F.R. §§ 825.104, 825.105. A corporation was not an FMLA employer where it did not employ 50 or more employees for each working day during each of 20 or more calendar workweeks in the current or preceding calendar year. *Sousa v. Orient Arts, Inc.*, 1999 WL 147724, 5 Wage & Hour Cas.2d (BNA) 383 (S.D.N.Y.1999). These statutory requirements are applicable even though an employer formally adopts the FMLA's provisions by adding a policy to its employee handbook. *Douglas v. E.G. Baldwin & Associates*, 150 F.3d 604 (6th Cir.1998); see also *Muller v. The Hotsy Corporation*, 917 F.Supp. 1389 (N.D.Iowa 1996).

Employment by distinctly different employers cannot be combined to create FMLA employer coverage. 29 C.F.R. § 825.106; see *Rollins v. Wilson County Government*, 967 F.Supp. 990 (M.D.Tenn. 1997); see also *Kilcrease v. Coffee County, Alabama*,

951 F.Supp. 212 (M.D.Ala.1996) (a county, rather than a sheriff, may have been a corrections officer's employer for the FMLA's purposes).

Courts have split on whether Congress intended to abrogate the states' Eleventh Amendment immunity under the FMLA. 29 U.S.C.A. § 2611(4)(B); 29 C.F.R. § 825.108. States and their political subdivisions are subject to suits by private citizens in federal court for FMLA violations. The Eleventh Amendment did not bar a state police officer's claims against the state police and state police officials in their official capacities for their alleged FMLA violations in denying him parental leave following his daughter's birth. *Knussman v. State of Maryland*, 935 F.Supp. 659 (D.Md.1996).

The Eleventh Amendment, however, barred a state employee's FMLA action against the Kansas Department of Human Resources. *Post v. Kansas, Department of Human Resources*, 1998 WL 928677, 5 Wage & Hour Cas.2d (BNA) 314 (D.Kan.1998). The court found that Congress did not effectively abrogate the states' Eleventh Amendment immunity in adopting the FMLA. See also *McGregor v. Goord*, 18 F. Supp.2d 204 (N.D.N.Y.1998) (even though Congress has provided clear legislative intent to abrogate the states' Eleventh Amendment immunity under the FMLA, the FMLA was not properly enacted pursuant to Congress' power under the Fourteenth Amendment).

14. EMPLOYER NOTICE

The FMLA and its regulations require an employer to notify employees of their FMLA leave rights through postings, written policies, etc. 29 U.S.C.A. § 2619; 29 C.F.R. §§ 825.300, 825.301.

a. Adequate Employer Notice

The FMLA's employer notice requirements can be satisfied where the employer posts the FMLA notice in employee break rooms, sets forth an FMLA policy in the employment handbook, and discusses it in employee risk management sessions. *Kaylor v. Fannin Regional Hospital*, 946 F.Supp. 988 (N.D.Ga. 1996). However, an employer's failure to present evidence that it posted the required FMLA notice did not prohibit the employer from terminating an employee. *Satterfield v. Wal–Mart Stores*, 135 F.3d 973 (5th Cir.1998), *reh'g en banc. denied*, 140 F.3d 1040 (5th Cir.1998). The employee failed to give notice of her need for leave under the FMLA. The FMLA's regulations do not place the burden of proving compliance with the posting requirements on the employer. The regulations prohibiting an employer that has failed to post the required notice from taking an adverse action against an employee applies only when the employee is required to provide advance notice of the need for FMLA leave. It does not apply to situations where the employee's need for leave is unforeseeable as in this case.

b. Inadequate Employer Notice

The FMLA notice must be conspicuously posted by the employer in a place where employees can reasonably expect the notice to be placed. *In-Sink–Erator v. Department of Industry, Labor and Human Relations*, 547 N.W.2d 792 (Wis.Ct.App.1996), *review denied*, 549 N.W.2d 734 (Wis.1996). Failure to make the required FMLA postings can effect an employer's ability to take adverse actions against an employee.

The FMLA's regulations provide that an employer who fails to provide written notice concerning employee rights and obligations cannot take an adverse action against an employee for failing to comply with any provision required to be set forth in the notice. An employer's admitted failure to post the required FMLA notice precluded it from claiming that the employee should have known of his FMLA rights. *Knussman v. Maryland*, 16 F. Supp.2d 601 (D.Md.1998). Likewise, an employer that never informed an employee of his FMLA rights and obligations could not claim that an employee forfeited his FMLA rights when he failed to report for work the day after his father's death. *Sherry v. Protection, Inc.*, 981 F.Supp. 1133 (N.D.Ill. 1997). In the absence of proper FMLA notice, an employee was entitled to twelve weeks of FMLA leave plus five days of paid vacation leave. See *Cline v. Wal–Mart Stores*, 144 F.3d 294 (4th Cir.1998).

Failure to give adequate FMLA notice can affect the employer's right to request medical certifications. An employer was not entitled to a summary judgment where the employee failed to provide a medical certification that he was needed to care for his wife. *Williams v. Shenango, Inc.*, 986 F.Supp. 309 (W.D.Pa.1997). There was no evidence that the employee was notified to provide a medical certification. See also *Stubl v. T.A. Systems, Inc.*, 984 F.Supp. 1075 (E.D.Mich.1997) (employer failed to provide notice for FMLA medical certification and to post FMLA notice).

15. EMPLOYER RECORDKEEPING REQUIREMENTS

The FMLA and its regulations require that an employer make, keep, and preserve records pertaining to the FMLA. 29 U.S.C.A. § 2616; 29 C.F.R. § 825.500. An airline employer, however, that failed to keep records of time that a flight attendant spent working after the flight "blocked in" was still able to establish that the attendant was not an FMLA eligible employee. *Robinson-Scott v. Delta Airlines*, 4 F. Supp.2d 1183 (N.D.Ga.1998). It determined how much time the attendant spent working after the flight "blocked in" by multiplying the time she remained on board after the "block in" by the number of duty periods. This formula established that the attendant did not work the required 1,250 hours. See also *Cantrell v. Delta Airlines*, 2 F. Supp.2d 1460 (N.D.Ga.1998); *Rich v. Delta Air Lines, Inc.*, 921 F.Supp. 767 (N.D.Ga.1996).

16.   FMLA REGULATIONS' VALIDITY

The FMLA required the Department of Labor (DOL) to promulgate regulations. 29 U.S.C.A. § 2654. These final FMLA regulations were issued on January 6, 1995. 29 C.F.R. §§ 825.100–825.800. Since their adoption, these regulations have generated litigation over their validity.

The FMLA's regulation prohibiting an employee's waiver of FMLA rights was found valid. *Bluitt v. Eval Company of America*, 3 F. Supp.2d 761 (S.D.Tex.1998). A release where an employee agreed to dismiss her Civil Rights Act of 1964 (Title VII) claims and all other causes of action was not enforceable.

Other FMLA regulations, however, have been found invalid. For example, the FMLA's regulations where an employer that confirms FMLA eligibility when the leave's notice is received may not subsequently challenge the employee's eligibility were found invalid. *Seaman v. Downtown Partnership*, 991 F.Supp. 751 (D.Md.1998). These regulations contradict Congress' intent regarding employee eligibility. If the employee is in fact ineligible for FMLA leave, the employer cannot on its own action confer statutory FMLA status on the employee.

The FMLA's regulations under which an employer's failure to give prospective notice that an absence from work is being designated as FMLA leave precludes the leave from being counted against the employee's twelve week leave entitlement have also

212 LITIGATION UNDER (FMLA) Ch. 5

been found invalid. *Cox v. Autozone, Inc.*, 990
F.Supp. 1369 (M.D.Ala.1998). The regulations add
requirements that go beyond the FMLA. They are
inconsistent with the FMLA's purpose of protecting
employees who take twelve or fewer weeks of leave
in granting entitlements that were not given by
Congress. The regulations convert an employer's
right to require an employee to substitute employer-
provided paid leave for unpaid FMLA leave into an
employee entitlement to more than twelve weeks of
leave.

The Department of Labor (DOL) usurped the
legislature's and judiciary's constitutional authority
in making an employee eligible for FMLA leave
unless the employee is given notice of ineligibility
from the employer within two days after it receives
the employee's leave request. *Wolke v. Dreadnought
Marine, Inc.*, 954 F.Supp. 1133 (E.D.Va.1997).

17. FEDERAL COURT REMOVAL

FMLA actions may be removed from state court
to federal court. For example, an employee brought
negligent misrepresentation claims against the employer in state court. *Ladner v. Alexander & Alexander, Inc.*, 879 F.Supp. 598 (W.D.La.1995). She
then amended the complaint to include an FMLA
claim. The employer removed the action to federal
court. The employee moved to remand asserting
that although FMLA claims may be brought in state
court, they may not be removed once commenced in
state court. The court disagreed. It held that the

federal court had original jurisdiction over the FMLA claim and the matter was properly removed.

18. HEALTH CARE PROVIDER

The FMLA and its regulations define "health care provider." 29 U.S.C.A. § 2611(6); 29 C.F.R. § 825.800. Not all health professionals qualify as FMLA health providers. For example, a chiropractor was found not qualified as one "capable of providing health care services" within the FMLA's definition even though the FMLA's regulations include chiropractors who perform manual manipulation of the spine to correct a subluxation shown on an x-ray where these procedures were not performed on the employee. *Sievers v. Iowa Mutual Insurance Company*, 581 N.W.2d 633 (Iowa Sup.Ct. 1998); see also *Olsen v. Ohio Edison Company*, 979 F.Supp. 1159 (N.D.Ohio 1997).

19. INDIVIDUAL LIABILITY

Individual liability for adverse actions against an employee by an employer's directors, managers, supervisors, and other employees may be found under the FMLA. See *Rupnow v. TRC, Inc.*, 999 F.Supp. 1047 (N.D.Ohio 1998) (supervisors); *Beyer v. Elkay Manufacturing Company*, 1997 WL 587487, 4 Wage & Hour Cas.2d (BNA) 984 (N.D.Ill.1997) (supervisors); *Stubl v. T.A. Systems, Inc.*, 984 F.Supp. 1075 (E.D.Mich.1997) (employer's president and vice president); *Freemon v. Foley*, 911 F.Supp. 326

(N.D.Ill.1995) (supervisors). Contra *Finnell v. Department of Industry, Labor & Human Relations, Equal Rights Division*, 519 N.W.2d 731 (Ct.App. 1994) (supervisor cannot be held individually liable under the FMLA or a state fair employment practices statute).

20. INSURANCE COVERAGE

The FMLA requires an employer to maintain an employee's group health plan coverage while on leave. 29 U.S.C.A. § 2614(c); 29 C.F.R. § 825.209–825.213; see *Stubl v. T.A. Systems, Inc.*, 984 F.Supp. 1075 (E.D.Mich.1997).

21. INTERMITTENT LEAVE

Intermittent leave or leave on a reduced schedule may be taken under the FMLA. 29 U.S.C.A. § 2612(b); 29 C.F.R. §§ 825.118, 825.203–825.205. An employee who is eligible for intermittent FMLA leave need only establish eligibility for the first absence and not for each subsequent absence. *Barron v. Runyon*, 11 F. Supp.2d 676 (E.D.Va.1998) (because employee was an eligible employee on the first date he took intermittent leave, all of the leave he subsequently took for the same medical purpose, subject to the same notice, and within the same twelve month period was covered by the FMLA).

22.　JOINT EMPLOYMENT

The FMLA's regulations provide that when two or more businesses exercise some control over the employee's work or working conditions they may be joint employers. 29 C.F.R. § 825.106. Joint employment exists when a temporary agency supplies employees to the second employer. *Miller v. Defiance Metal Products*, 989 F.Supp. 945 (N.D.Ohio 1997) The employee's status as an FMLA eligible employee is determined from the date that the employee begins working at the company's facility and not from the date that the employee becomes the company's permanent employee.

Working for two different distinct employment entities, however, does not establish joint employment. Time that an employee worked for a county government could not be combined with the time she worked for a county board of education for determining the employee's FMLA eligibility. *Rollins v. Wilson County Government*, 154 F.3d 626 (6th Cir.1998).

A leased employee may not be jointly employed where the leasing agency does not exercise sufficient control over the employee to be considered an "employer." *Astrowsky v. First Portland Mortgage Corporation*, 887 F.Supp. 332 (D.Me.1995). This occurred where an employee was leased to a company for the long term and was essentially the company's permanent employee.

23. JURY TRIAL

An employee has a right to a jury trial under the FMLA. Even though the FMLA is silent on a jury trial, the FMLA's civil enforcement scheme mirrors the Fair Labor Standards Act's (FLSA's). The FMLA's legislative history indicated that Congress intended to align the FMLA's procedures with the FLSA's. However, claims relating to reinstatement or promotion will be resolved by the court, rather than a jury. These latter remedies deal with rights traditionally granted by an equity court and not a court of law. *Helmly v. Stone Container Corp.*, 957 F.Supp. 1274 (S.D.Ga.1997); see also *Frizzell v. Southwest Motor Freight*, 154 F.3d 641 (6th Cir. 1998) (FMLA provides for a jury trial right).

24. LEAVE CALCULATION

An employee may take up to twelve weeks of unpaid FMLA leave. 29 U.S.C.A. § 2612(a)(1); 29 C.F.R. § 825.200. The FMLA leave normally ends at the leave's expiration or when the event giving rise to the leave no longer exists. For example, FMLA leave ended with the person's death for whom the employee cared. *Brown v. J.C. Penney Corp.*, 924 F.Supp. 1158 (S.D.Fla.1996).

25. LEAVE DESIGNATION

It is the employer's responsibility to designate leave, paid or unpaid, as FMLA qualifying leave. 29 C.F.R. § 825.208. An employer violated the FMLA by retroactively designating vacation and sick days taken by an injured employee as FMLA leave. Where the employer has the knowledge to determine that the leave was FMLA, but fails to designate it as FMLA leave when it commences, the employer must wait until the employee is notified of this designation to begin the time period for the FMLA's twelve week limit. *Viereck v. City of Gloucester*, 961 F.Supp. 703 (D.N.J.1997).

26. LEAVE DONATION

The FMLA does not require an employer to permit an employee to use donated leave from other employees. An employee had no FMLA claim from an employer's refusal to allow her to use donated sick leave she had accrued prior to the sick leave donation program's termination. *Kilcrease v. Coffee County, Alabama*, 951 F.Supp. 212 (M.D.Ala.1996).

27. MEDICAL CERTIFICATIONS

The FMLA and its regulations permit an employer to require medical certifications under certain circumstances. 29 U.S.C.A. § 2613; 29 C.F.R. §§ 825.305–825.311. To request a medical examination, the employer must formally notify the employee.

An employee's medical examination, however, that occurred after he commenced leave was sufficient to bring him within the FMLA's protection even though the employer's internal procedures indicated that medical evidence must be submitted to the employer before a medical leave would be granted. *Stubl v. T.A. Systems, Inc.*, 984 F.Supp. 1075 (E.D.Mich.1997). The employer did not comply with the FMLA's regulations. It failed to provide notice for this certification and to post the FMLA notice. See also *Williams v. Shenango, Inc.*, 986 F.Supp. 309 (W.D.Pa.1997) (no evidence that the employee was notified to provide a medical certification).

The initial certification must be performed by the employee's own physician. The United States Postal Service (USPS) could not require a district manager, who had taken a leave of absence to submit to a fitness for duty examination, including a psychiatric evaluation, with a doctor it designated. The FMLA requires the employer to rely on an evaluation done by the employee's clinician. The letter from the manager's doctor certifying her fit to return to work as long as the USPS made necessary changes to assure her of freedom from harassment and discrimination satisfied the FMLA's fitness for duty standard. *Albert v. Runyon*, 6 F. Supp.2d 57 (D.Mass.1998). If the USPS believed that the doctor's proviso against alleged harassment indicated limitations on the manager's ability to work, it should have sought a clarification from the doctor.

If the employer is not satisfied with the medical certification it can request a second opinion. An employer properly sent a notice requiring an employee on FMLA leave to obtain a second opinion medical examination to the employee's last address of record. *Diaz v. Fort Wayne Foundry Corporation*, 131 F.3d 711 (7th Cir.1997).

The employer cannot use an employer-associated doctor for the examination. The FMLA expressly prohibits the use of an employer-associated doctor for a second opinion. A city could not use the city doctor's opinion in determining if an employee who requested leave was fit to work. *Price v. Fort Wayne*, 117 F.3d 1022 (7th Cir.1997). However, a hospital did not violate the FMLA when it requested a technician to obtain a second opinion from a psychiatrist who rented office space in the hospital but was never employed by the hospital. *Yousuf v. UHS of De La Ronde, Inc.*, 1999 WL 109565, 5 Wage & Hour Cas.2d 353 (E.D.La.1999).

If an employee fails to return to work with a properly requested FMLA medical certification, the employee can be terminated. An employer did not violate the FMLA when it terminated an employee who failed to return to work at the end of a twelve week leave period ready to work and with the requisite certification of fitness for duty. *Nunes v. Wal–Mart Stores*, 980 F.Supp. 1336 (N.D.Cal.1997).

The FMLA was not violated when an employer terminated an employee for excessive absences after the employee's doctor certified that the employee, who suffered from chronic fatigue syndrome, was not presently incapacitated and could return to work. *Stoops v. One Call Communications*, 141 F.3d

309 (7th Cir.1998). No merit was found in the employee's contention that once he called in sick that the employer was required to investigate further and require a doctor's certification if it wanted verification of his condition. Once the employee said that he was missing work because of chronic fatigue syndrome, he was providing a reason that the employer knew that the doctor had concluded was not a qualifying FMLA leave reason. If the employee knew the doctor's initial certification was wrong, it was the employee's burden to have it corrected. The employee did nothing to obtain a contrary opinion either from that doctor or another one.

28.   NO–FAULT ATTENDANCE POLICIES

An employer cannot count FMLA absences under a no-fault attendance policy. 29 C.F.R. § 825.220(c). An employer's no-fault attendance policy violated the FMLA. *George v. Associated Stationers*, 932 F.Supp. 1012 (N.D.Ohio 1996). Any absence other than that taken within vacation time was characterized as an occurrence and counted in the point system for taking disciplinary action. The attendance policy did not except an absence caused by a serious health condition.

An employee's daughter who had a "serious health condition" could not be terminated. *Brannon v. OshKosh B'Gosh, Inc.*, 897 F.Supp. 1028 (M.D.Tenn.1995). The employee should not have been assessed absence points for her absence.

29. PAID LEAVE SUBSTITUTION

Prior to taking an FMLA leave, an employer must give the employee notice that paid leave will be designated as part of the FMLA leave. 29 U.S.C.A. § 2612(d)(2); 29 C.F.R. §§ 825.207(b), 825.207(c), 825.207(e), 825.207(f), 825.208(c). A store manager who received employer-provided disability pay for thirteen of fifteen weeks of leave stated no FMLA claim. *Cline v. Wal–Mart Stores*, 144 F.3d 294 (4th Cir.1998). The FMLA provides protection only when the employee takes twelve or fewer weeks of leave. The manager took more than twelve weeks of leave. She collected disability pay while on leave and the employer properly counted that paid leave against her FMLA entitlement. The FMLA allows an employee to elect or the employer to substitute accrued paid leave for unpaid FMLA leave. This provision exists so that employees may not be told that leave must be taken as unpaid when an alternative employer-provided paid leave may be taken. The FMLA does not require that the employee be given twelve unpaid weeks of leave in addition to the paid weeks provided by the employer. See also *Cox v. Autozone, Inc.*, 990 F.Supp. 1369 (M.D.Ala.1998).

The employer cannot retroactively designate vacation and sick days taken by an employee as FMLA leave. 29 C.F.R. § 825.208(c). An employer that has the requisite knowledge to determine that a leave is FMLA, but fails to designate it as FMLA leave when the leave commences, must wait until the employee is notified of this designation for the time period to begin on the FMLA's twelve week limit for unpaid leaves. *Viereck v. City of Gloucester*, 961 F.Supp. 703 (D.N.J.1997).

30.   PREEMPTION

Courts are split on whether the at-will employment doctrine's public policy exception preempts the FMLA. For example, a retaliatory termination suit based on a claim for exercising FMLA rights was rejected. *Hamros v. Bethany Homes and Methodist Hospital of Chicago*, 894 F.Supp. 1176 (N.D.Ill.1995). The employee was terminated while on medical leave to obtain therapy for clinical depression. The employee filed suit alleging that the hospital's actions violated a clear public policy mandate and that the suit should be recognized under the state's employment-at-will doctrine's retaliatory termination exception. The court refused to expand the retaliatory termination tort to cover FMLA claims because the FMLA already provided adequate remedies for retaliation. See also *Gall v. Quaker City Castings, Inc.*, 874 F.Supp. 161 (N.D.Ohio 1995) (availability of the FMLA's statutory or administrative remedies precluded wrongful termination cause of action based on a public policy violation).

The FMLA, however, did not completely preempt a former bus driver's wrongful termination claim. *Danfelt v. Board of County Commissioners*, 998 F.Supp. 606 (D.Md.1998). There was no meaningful conflict between the FMLA and Maryland's wrongful termination law. The court found that the FMLA's savings clause did not completely preempt state tort law.

31.   PREGNANCY

The FMLA and its regulations permit an employee to take leave for the birth of a daughter or son. 29 U.S.C.A. § 2612(a)(1)(A); 29 C.F.R. § 825.112(a)(1). An employee's failure to provide evidence from a health care provider that her morning sickness rendered her unable to perform her job functions was not fatal to her FMLA claim. *Pendarvis v. Xerox Corporation*, 3 F. Supp.2d 53 (D.D.C. 1998). Neither the FMLA or its regulations require this evidence in cases of pregnancy-related morning sickness. Pregnancy is treated in the regulations differently from other serious health conditions. See 29 C.F.R. § 825.114(e). In absence of the employer's request for medical certification, the regulations that specifically address pregnancy and related conditions cannot be reconciled with the requirement that pregnant employees must always provide medical evidence that they are unable to work due to morning sickness.

32.   REINSTATEMENT

a.   **Equivalent Position**

Upon return from an FMLA leave, the FMLA and its regulations require that the employer reinstate the employee to the "same" or "equivalent" position. 29 U.S.C.A. § 2614(a)(1); 29 C.F.R. §§ 825.214–825.216. For example, an employee was restored to her former position as House Producer for the employer's news show. *Lempres v. CBS, Inc.*, 916 F.Supp. 15 (D.D.C.1996).

Where the same position is not available, the FMLA entitles employers to return employees not to the position they left before taking the leave, but to an equivalent position. *Brown v. J.C. Penney Corp.*, 924 F.Supp. 1158 (S.D.Fla.1996). A headquarters secretary's position was equivalent to a field secretary. *Vargas v. Globetrotters Engineering*, 4 F. Supp.2d 780 (N.D.Ill.1998).

Employers have violated the FMLA where employees where not reinstated to equivalent positions. An employee was not reinstated to the same or equivalent position, but was placed on probation, discriminated against, and terminated for exercising FMLA rights. *Blackwell v. Harris Chemical*, 11 F. Supp.2d 1302 (D.Kan.1998).

Genuine issues of material fact existed whether the third shift attendant position and an office job were equivalent. *Watkins v. J & S Oil Company*, 977 F.Supp. 520 (D.Me.1997). The employee held a manager position before the leave.

A former warehouse manager was returned to a position as a salary-paid warehouse coordinator. *Lloyd v. Wyoming Valley Health Care*, 994 F.Supp. 288 (M.D.Pa.1998). The employee eventually became a corporate sales representative receiving salary plus commission. This change in the compensation raised genuine issues concerning the employee's future tangible economic loss. The manager provided evidence that his vacation and sick pay were devalued by at least ten percent due to the change.

b. Failure to Reinstate

An employer is required to reinstate the employee upon the FMLA leave's completion. 29 U.S.C.A. § 2614(a)(1); 29 C.F.R. §§ 825.214–825.216. The FMLA was violated when an employer failed to restore an employee to his prior position upon return to work prior to the FMLA leave's expiration. *Cline v. Wal–Mart Stores*, 144 F.3d 294 (4th Cir. 1998).

However, an employer was not required to reinstate an employee to her billing manager position when she returned from an FMLA leave. *Hubbard v. Blue Cross Blue Shield*, 1 F. Supp.2d 867 (N.D.Ill. 1998). The employee would have been terminated for poor work performance even if she had not taken leave. Prior to taking leave, the employee had been placed on a corrective action program. The employer presented evidence that the employee failed to meet the program's goals. The employee did not offer any evidence that she was performing well in the areas that prompted her termination.

No FMLA rights existed in an employee's restoration to her position as a hospital's director of human resources. *Tardie v. Rehabilitation Hospital of Rhode Island*, 168 F.3d 538 (1st Cir.1999). Her ability to work extended hours was an essential function of the position. The employee who was unable to work more than forty hours per week could not effectively perform her job's functions.

c. Layoff

Employees legitimately laid-off during an FMLA leave are not entitled to be reinstated upon the leave's completion. 29 C.F.R. § 825.216(a)(1). An employer articulated a legitimate nondiscriminatory reason for terminating an employee. *Hodgens v. General Dynamics Corporation*, 144 F.3d 151 (1st Cir.1998). The reduction in force was legitimate and economically necessary. The employee's performance was below par and significantly lower than the performance of all similarly situated employees.

A laid-off employee, however, was permitted to claim reinstatement. *Duckworth v. Pratt & Whitney, Inc.*, 152 F.3d 1 (1st Cir.1998). The employer refused to rehire the laid-off employee because he had a poor attendance rating resulting from an FMLA protected absence.

33.   REQUIRING FMLA LEAVE

Nothing under the FMLA prevents an employer from requiring an employee to take FMLA leave where it is available. The FMLA was not violated when an employer placed a pregnant lab technician on FMLA leave, even though the technician did not request the leave. *Harvender v. Norton Company*, 1997 WL 793085, 4 Wage & Hour Cas.2d (BNA) 560

(N.D.N.Y.1997). The employer had been presented with a medical opinion that the technician could not be exposed to chemicals, which was an essential job element. The employer was permitted to characterize the employee's absence as FMLA leave.

34. RETALIATORY ACTIONS

Employers cannot retaliate against employees for exercising or failing to exercise any FMLA rights. 29 U.S.C.A. § 2615; 29 C.F.R. § 825.220.

a. Burden of Proof

The shifting burden proof analysis of *McDonnell Douglas Corp. v. Green*, 411 U.S. 792 (1973), applies to FMLA claims making it unlawful for an employer to terminate or discriminate against any individual for opposing any FMLA practice. *Williams v. Shenango, Inc.*, 986 F.Supp. 309 (W.D.Pa.1997). To establish a prima facie FMLA retaliation case, the plaintiff must show that he or she availed himself or herself of a protected FMLA right, was adversely affected by an employment decision, and there was a causal connection between the protected activity and the adverse employment action. *Hodgens v. General Dynamics Corporation*, 144 F.3d 151 (1st Cir.1998); see also *Leary v. Hobet Mining*, 981 F.Supp. 452 (S.D.W.Va.1997).

A city housing authority's former police supervisor who claimed that the authority's chief of police and director of human resources retaliated against him for complaining to the Department of Labor

(DOL) stated a claim. *Blumenthal v. Murray*, 995 F.Supp. 831 (S.D.Ill.1998). He alleged that he was terminated, that his benefits were terminated or modified without notice or justification, that information concerning his rights under COBRA was intentionally withheld, and that his medical expenses were not paid.

An employee sufficiently plead FMLA violations. *Blackwell v. Harris Chemical*, 11 F. Supp.2d 1302 (D.Kan.1998). She alleged that when she returned from an FMLA leave that she was not reinstated to the same or equivalent position, was placed on probation, discriminated against, and was terminated for exercising FMLA rights.

An employee attempting to establish an FMLA claim through circumstantial evidence may establish a prima facie case by using the so-called: (1) discriminatory framework under which the employee must prove that he or she was a member of a protected class, suffered an adverse job action, was qualified for the position he or she was holding, and another employee who did not exercise rights under the FMLA was treated more favorably or (2) retaliatory framework under which the employee must prove he or she availed himself or herself of the protected FMLA rights, suffered an adverse job action, and there was a causal connection with the assertion of the FMLA right. *Peters v. Community Action Committee*, 977 F.Supp. 1428 (M.D.Ala. 1997).

The burden-shifting analytical framework used in the Civil Rights Act of 1964 (Title VII) actions should be used when an FMLA plaintiff's evidence is based upon circumstantial evidence of an employer's alleged discriminatory intent. However, a restaurant did not violate the FMLA when it demoted a dining room supervisor while she was on an FMLA leave. The supervisor failed to show that the restaurant's legitimate nondiscriminatory reasons for the demotion, namely her inadequate work performance and need for supervisory changes to improve product quality and customer satisfaction, were pretextual. *Dollar v. Shoney's, Inc.*, 981 F.Supp. 1417 (N.D.Ala.1997).

b. Evidence

The standard applied in determining whether a violation of the Fair Labor Standards Act (FLSA) is willful is whether the employer knew or showed reckless disregard for whether its conduct was prohibited by the FLSA applies in the FMLA's context. The FMLA and the FLSA are governed by virtually identical limitations schemes. An employee's complaint was sufficient where it alleged that the employer willfully interfered with his FMLA leave by forcing him to take physical therapy on his own time and by terminating him for exercising FMLA leave rights. The employee's action was timely filed within the three year limitations period for willful FMLA violations. *Settle v. S.W. Rodgers Company*, 998 F.Supp. 657 (E.D.Va.1998).

Likewise, the burden-shifting analytical framework applied under the Civil Rights Act of 1964 (Title VII) should be used when an FMLA plaintiff's evidence is based upon circumstantial evidence of an employer's alleged discriminatory intent. However, a restaurant did not violate the FMLA when it demoted the dining room supervisor while she was on an FMLA leave. The supervisor failed to show that the restaurant's legitimate nondiscriminatory reasons for the demotion, namely her inadequate work performance and need for supervisory changes to improve product quality and customer satisfaction, were pretextual. *Dollar v. Shoney's, Inc.*, 981 F.Supp. 1417 (N.D.Ala.1997).

c. Types of Retaliation

An employee was permitted to maintain an action against an employer for retaliation where the employer terminated the employee for asserting FMLA rights. *Cline v. Wal–Mart Stores*, 144 F.3d 294 (4th Cir.1998). Terminating an employee prior to beginning an FMLA leave may be retaliation. *Dumoulin v. Formica*, 968 F.Supp. 68 (N.D.N.Y.1997). Reassignment to a new position with a pay reduction may constitute retaliation. *Peters v. Community Ac-*

tion Committee, 977 F.Supp. 1428 (M.D.Ala.1997). Demoting an employee upon return to work may raise retaliation issues. *Sherry v. Protection, Inc.*, 981 F.Supp. 1133 (N.D.Ill.1997). Taking an adverse action against an employee through a disciplinary suspension raises retaliation concerns. *Williams v. Shenango, Inc.*, 986 F.Supp. 309 (W.D.Pa.1997). Laying off an employee upon return from an FMLA leave may be considered retaliation. *Vanderhoof v. Life Extension Institute*, 988 F.Supp. 507 (D.N.J. 1997).

Retaliation for exercising FMLA rights has not been found where an employer terminated an employee who suffered from hypertension and atrial fibrillation and who chose to remain out of work for a six week period. *Hodgens v. General Dynamics*, 144 F.3d 151 (1st Cir.1998). Even if the employee's condition qualified as a serious health condition, there was no evidence that his condition rendered him unable to perform his position's function. The employee's doctor found that the employee was able to continue working. Retaliation has not been found where an employee failed to give notice of the need for FMLA leave. *Satterfield v. Wal–Mart Stores*, 135 F.3d 973 (5th Cir.1998).

35. SERIOUS HEALTH CONDITION

The FMLA and its regulations define a "serious health condition" in considerable detail. 29 U.S.C.A. § 2611(11); 29 C.F.R. § 825.114. The following claims have been asserted to determine whether a serious health condition existed:

a. Asthma

Asthma can be a serious health condition. *Beal v. Rubbermaid Commercial Products, Inc.*, 972 F.Supp. 1216 (S.D.Iowa 1997). Depending upon the circumstances, however, asthma may not be a serious health condition. *Rhoads v. Federal Deposit Insurance Corp.*, 956 F.Supp. 1239 (D.Md.1997); *Sakellarion v. Judge & Dolph, Ltd.*, 893 F.Supp. 800 (N.D.Ill.1995).

b. Back Injuries

A general back injury is not a serious health condition. *Beal v. Rubbermaid Commercial Products*, 972 F.Supp. 1216 (S.D.Iowa 1997); *Olsen v. Ohio Edison Company*, 979 F.Supp. 1159 (N.D.Ohio 1997). An employee's degenerative back condition, however, qualified as a serious health condition. *Kaylor v. Fannin Regional Hospital*, 946 F.Supp. 988 (N.D.Ga.1996).

c. Bronchitis

Bronchitis is not a serious health condition where the employee is not incapacitated and receives no continuing treatment by a health care provider. *Beal v. Rubbermaid Commercial Products, Inc.*, 972 F.Supp. 1216 (S.D.Iowa 1997).

d. Carpal Tunnel Syndrome

An employee's manifestation of carpal tunnel syndrome was not a serious health condition, even though carpal tunnel syndrome if sufficiently severe could be a serious health condition. *Price v. Mara-*

thon Cheese Corporation, 119 F.3d 330 (5th Cir. 1997).

e. Chicken Pox

Chicken pox is a serious health condition. *George v. Associated Stationers*, 932 F.Supp. 1012 (N.D.Ohio 1996).

f. Chronic Fatigue Syndrome

Chronic fatigue syndrome is not a serious health condition. *Stoops v. One Call Communications*, 141 F.3d 309 (7th Cir.1998).

g. Diabetes

Diabetes is a serious health condition. *Beal v. Rubbermaid Commercial Products, Inc.*, 972 F.Supp. 1216 (S.D.Iowa 1997).

h. Ear Infection (Otitis Media)

An ear infection is not a serious health condition. *Seidle v. Provident Mutual Life Ins. Co.*, 871 F.Supp. 238 (E.D.Pa.1994).

i. Eczema (Skin Condition)

Eczema is not a serious health condition. *Beal v. Rubbermaid Commercial Products, Inc.*, 972 F.Supp. 1216 (S.D.Iowa 1997).

j. Food Poisoning

Food poisoning is not a serious health condition. *Oswalt v. Sara Lee Corp.*, 74 F.3d 91 (5th Cir.1996).

k. General Illness

A general illness that incapacitates an individual is not covered by the FMLA. *Satterfield v. Wal–Mart Stores, Inc.*, 135 F.3d 973 (5th Cir.1998); *Brannon v. OshKosh B'Gosh, Inc.*, 897 F.Supp. 1028 (M.D.Tenn.1995); *Carter v. Rental Uniform Service*, 977 F.Supp. 753 (W.D.Va.1997).

l. Grief and Despair

A serious health condition contemplates only a medical condition affecting the living. An employee, however, who claimed that he was entitled to an FMLA leave due to the "grief and despair" suffered following his mother's death was permitted to amend his complaint if he could support a claim that he suffered from a serious health condition. *Lange v. Showbiz Pizza Time*, 12 F.Supp.2d 1150 (D.Kan.1998). An employer, however, properly terminated an employee for failing to return from leave following his father's death. *Fisher v. State Farm Mut. Auto. Insurance*, 999 F.Supp. 866 (E.D.Tex.1998). The doctor stated he could perform activities of daily living during the leave period.

m. Headaches

Migraine headaches may be a serious health condition. See *Vargo-Adams v. United States Postal Service*, 992 F.Supp. 939 (N.D.Ohio 1998); *Hendry v. GTE North, Inc.*, 896 F.Supp. 816 (N.D.Ind.1995).

n. High Blood Pressure (Hypertension)

Hypertension absent incapacitation that prevents an employee from performing his or her duties is insufficient to establish a serious health condition. See *Hodgens v. General Dynamics*, 144 F.3d 151 (1st Cir.1998); *Austin v. Shelby County Government*, 1999 WL 95990, 5 Wage & Hour Cas.2d (BNA) 375 (Tenn.Ct.App.1999).

o. Menstrual Bleeding

Menstrual bleeding may not qualify as a serious health condition. *Roberts v. Human Development Association*, 4 F. Supp.2d 154 (E.D.N.Y.1998).

p. Morning Sickness

Morning sickness may qualify as a serious health condition. *Pendarvis v. Xerox Corporation*, 3 F. Supp.2d 53 (D.D.C.1998).

q. Motor Vehicle Accident

Injuries resulting from a motor vehicle accident may be sufficient in scope to constitute a serious health condition. *Viereck v. Gloucester City*, 961 F.Supp. 703 (D.N.J.1997).

r. Multiple Diagnosis

If temporarily linked, several diagnoses, no one of which arises alone to the level of a serious health condition can, if taken together, constitute a serious health condition. An employee with a multiple diagnosis, including elevated blood pressure, hyperthyroidism, back pain, severe headaches, sinusitis, infected cyst, sore and swelling throat, coughing, and stress and depression, submitted enough evidence to withstand a summary judgment on a claim that she did not suffer from a serious health condition under the FMLA. *Price v. Fort Wayne*, 117 F.3d 1022 (7th Cir.1997). The employee's doctor swore in an affidavit that she was on the edge of a physical and mental breakdown and that there was no way she could perform her job due to her physical and mental state.

s. Poison Ivy

Poison ivy is not a serious health condition where an employee received treatment for it only on one occasion, no medication was prescribed, and nothing indicated that the employee was incapacitated due to it. *Godwin v. Rheem Manufacturing Co.*, 15 F. Supp.2d 1197 (M.D.Ala.1998).

t. Rectal Bleeding

Rectal bleeding, possibly caused by hemorrhoids, was not a serious health condition. *Bauer v. Varity Dayton–Walther Corp.*, 118 F.3d 1109 (6th Cir. 1997).

u. Respiratory Infections

Respiratory infections are not a serious health condition. *Murray v. Red Kap Industries*, 124 F.3d 695 (5th Cir.1997).

v. Sexual Harassment

Sexual harassment may rise to the level of a serious health condition. An employee who alleged that as a result of assault and other episodes of sexual harassment by her supervisors that she required medical attention gave the employer sufficient notice of claims for a serious health condition.

Vasconcellos v. Cybex International, 962 F.Supp. 701 (D.Md.1997). The serious health condition included shock, tremors, panic attacks, severe chest pains, and an inability to breathe. These affected her mental and physical health and rendered her unable to perform her job functions for more than three days.

w. Sexual Molestation

An employee's child who was suspected of being sexually molested did not have a serious health condition. *Martyszenko v. Safeway*, 120 F.3d 120 (8th Cir.1997).

x. Shoulder Injury

A shoulder injury may constitute a serious health condition. *Santos v. Shields Health Group*, 996 F.Supp. 87 (D.Mass.1998).

y. Sinobronchitis

Sinobronchitis is not a serious health condition. *Hott v. VDO Yazaki Corp.*, 922 F.Supp. 1114 (W.D.Va.1996).

z. Tendinitis

Tendinitis is not a serious health condition. *Bond v. Abbott Laboratories*, 7 F. Supp.2d 967 (N.D.Ohio 1998).

aa. Toothache

Routine tooth extractions are not a serious health condition. *Bond v. Abbott Laboratories*, 7 F. Supp.2d 967 (N.D.Ohio 1998).

ab. Ulcers

Ulcers may be a serious health condition. *Victorelli v. Shadyside Hospital*, 128 F.3d 184 (3d Cir. 1997). A mild ulcer, however, is not a serious health condition. *Thorson v. Gemini, Inc.*, 123 F.3d 1140 (8th Cir.1997), *on remand summ. judgment granted*, 998 F.Supp. 1034 (N.D.Iowa 1998).

ac. Upset Stomach (Gastroenteritis)

Even though the FMLA's regulations list upset stomach and minor ulcers as examples of conditions that do not meet a serious health condition's definition, the Department of Labor (DOL) issued an opinion letter providing that if the conditions listed in the regulations met the regulatory criteria for a serious health condition that the absence could be FMLA protected. *Thorson v. Gemini, Inc.*, 123 F.3d 1140 (8th Cir.1997), *on remand summ. judgment granted*, 998 F.Supp. 1034 (N.D.Iowa 1998). An employee's upset stomach, however, was not a serious health condition. *Brannon v. OshKosh B'Gosh, Inc.*, 897 F.Supp. 1028 (M.D.Tenn.1995). Likewise, a stomach virus was not a serious health condition. *Kaylor v. Fannin Regional Hospital, Inc.*, 946 F.Supp. 988 (N.D.Ga.1996).

36.   SICK LEAVE

Under the FMLA, an employee may elect or an employer may require that paid sick leave be substituted for unpaid FMLA leave where the leave is for the employee's serious health condition or to care for a family member's serious health condition. 29 U.S.C.A. § 2612(d)(2)(B); 29 C.F.R. §§ 825.207(c); 825.208(c). An employer's sick leave policy and its use cannot conflict with the FMLA. However, nothing in the FMLA prohibits an employer from making a family member's residency in the employee's household a condition for paid sick leave receipt. *Rock Island County,* 104 Lab. Arb. (BNA) 1127 (1995) (Witney, Arb.).

37. STATUTE OF LIMITATIONS

The FMLA provides that an action may be brought under it within two years for a nonwillful violation and within three years for a willful violation. 29 U.S.C.A. § 2617(c).

a. Nonwillful Violations

A nonwillful violation arose where an employer's alleged FMLA violation was its failure to designate an employee's workers' compensation leave as FMLA leave. *Moore v. Payless Shoe Source,* 139 F.3d 1210 (8th Cir.1998). This claim was time barred where it occurred and accrued in September 1993 when the employee began her medical leave, but the employee's complaint was not filed until December 1995. The employee did not allege willful misconduct for applying the three year statute of limitations instead of the two year statute of limitations for a nonwillful violation. See also *Shannon v. City of Philadelphia,* 1999 WL 126097, 5 Wage & Hour Cas.2d (BNA) 380 (E.D.Pa.1999) (applying two year statute of limitations).

b. Willful Violations

The standard applied in determining whether a willful FMLA violation has occurred is that used under the Fair Labor Standards Act (FLSA). *Settle v. S.W. Rodgers Company*, 998 F.Supp. 657 (E.D.Va. 1998). This standard is applied in the FMLA's context because the FMLA and the FLSA are governed by virtually identical limitations schemes.

Under the FLSA, conduct is willful where the employer knew or showed reckless disregard for whether its conduct was prohibited by the FLSA. An employee's complaint alleging that the employer willfully interfered with his FMLA right to unpaid leave by forcing him to take physical therapy on his own time and by terminating him in retaliation for exercising FMLA leave rights was timely filed within the three year limitations period for willful FMLA violations. *Settle v. S.W. Rodgers Company*, 998 F.Supp. 657 (E.D.Va.1998); see also *Shannon v. City of Philadelphia*, 1999 WL 126097, 5 Wage & Hour Cas.2d (BNA) 380 (E.D.Pa.1999) (applying three year statute of limitations).

38.   SUCCESSOR EMPLOYER

The FMLA and its regulations define an employer to include "any successor in interest." 29 U.S.C.A. § 2611(4)(A)(ii)(II);   29   C.F.R.   §§ 825.104(a); 825.107. In determining whether an employer is a "successor in interest," the court will look to the FMLA's regulations and at court decisions arising under the Civil Rights Act of 1964 (Title VII) and the Labor Management Relations Act (LMRA). *Vanderhoof v. Life Extension Institute*, 988 F.Supp. 507 (D.N.J.1997).

A company that purchased certain of an employer's assets was a successor employer under the FMLA. *Vanderhoof v. Life Extension Institute*, 988 F.Supp. 507 (D.N.J.1997). The company acquired clinics, their related contracts, machinery, equipment, furniture, inventories, leases, books, documents, and medical records. It continued to provide the same types of services as had the prior employer. All workers at the clinic were rehired after the purchase. A change in upper management did not cause a substantial transformation in basic operations and the types of services offered remained the same. It was irrelevant that employees in other clinics were not rehired. The other clinics were subsequently closed and the company changed its focus regarding clients to whom it provided services.

39. UNEMPLOYMENT COMPENSATION

Unemployment compensation claims may arise out of an FMLA leave. These may be based upon an employee's termination for exercising FMLA rights, not returning from leave, failing to follow employer reporting procedures, refusing to obtain a medical certification, etc. An employee, however, was ineligible for unemployment compensation where the employee voluntarily resigned. *Thompson v. Unemployment Comp. Bd.*, 687 A.2d 1 (Pa.Cmwlth.Ct. 1996). She ignored repeated requests following expiration of her FMLA leave that she complete the employer's form for a medical/personal leave of absence.

40. WAIVER OF FMLA RIGHTS

The FMLA's regulations prohibit an employee from waiving or an employer from inducing an employee to waive FMLA rights. 29 C.F.R. § 825.220(d). This regulation has been found to be valid. *Bluitt v. Eval Company of America*, 3 F. Supp.2d 761 (S.D.Tex.1998). A release was not enforced where an employee agreed to dismiss claims under the Civil Rights Act of 1964 (Title VII) and to release the employer from all causes of action.

CHAPTER 6

DRAFTING FAMILY AND MEDICAL LEAVE ACT (FMLA) PROCEDURES, POLICIES, AND FORMS

A. INTRODUCTION

Most employers understand that they are required to provide employees with the Family and Medical Leave Act's (FMLA's) leave and benefits. However, the FMLA and the Department of Labor's (DOL's) regulations present employers with a multitude of compliance issues in drafting procedures, policies, and forms to implement and administer its provisions. Pub. L. No. 103–3, 107 Stat. 6 (1993); *codified at* 2 U.S.C.A. §§ 1301, 1302, 1312, 1381–1385, 1401–1416; 5 U.S.C.A. §§ 6381–6387; 29 U.S.C.A. §§ 2601–2654; 29 C.F.R. §§ 825.100–825.800.

In drafting FMLA procedures, policies, and forms, the FMLA and its regulations must be understood. For example, the FMLA's interplay with the Americans with Disabilities Act (ADA), workers' compensation statutes, and state and local family and medical leave statutes must be considered. See 29 U.S.C.A. § 2651, 42 U.S.C.A. §§ 12101–17, 12201–13; 29 C.F.R. §§ 825.701–825–702.

The FMLA should be complied with and administered through proactive employer measures that:

1. Manage employee absenteeism;

2. Promote an employee's early return to work; and

3. Control benefit costs.

Implementing and administering the FMLA in this manner will lessen the possibility of an employer's liability for FMLA violations.

This chapter reviews considerations for implementing and administering FMLA requirements. To assist in better understanding these requirements, sample procedures, policies, and forms are provided for guidance.

B. IMPLEMENTING FMLA REQUIREMENTS

Before implementing the FMLA's requirements, an employer should obtain the answers to the following questions:

1. How does the FMLA compare with any state and/or local law? Consider the following:

    a. Is the FMLA more restrictive regarding leave and/or benefits?

    b. Is the FMLA less restrictive regarding leave and/or benefits?

2. How does the FMLA compare with the employer's current leave policies? Consider the following:

a. Are the employer's current leave policies more restrictive than the FMLA?

b. Are the employer's current leave policies less restrictive than the FMLA?

3. What are the FMLA's implications for group health plans? Consider the following:

a. Are the FMLA's provisions more restrictive?

b. Are the FMLA's provisions less restrictive?

Unless a collective bargaining agreement is in effect or other employment contracts exist that specify employment terms and conditions for an individual employee or an employee group, the employer may unilaterally change policies and benefits as it deems appropriate. Benefits can be increased or decreased as long as they do not fall below any federal, state, or local requirements. See 29 U.S.C.A. §§ 2652–2653; 29 C.F.R. § 825.700. However, these changes cannot adversely affect an employee who is currently on FMLA leave. The changes can only be prospective and not retroactive. See 29 U.S.C.A. §§ 2652–2653; 29 C.F.R. § 825.700.

In implementing and administering the FMLA, the employer should consider:

1. The minimum obligations of federal, state, and/or local law;

2. The level of group health plan benefits that the employer desires to provide;

3. The cost of providing any group health plan benefits beyond what is required by federal, state, and/or local law;

4. The ease of administration; and

5. The cost of administration.

C. PERMISSIBLE AND NONPERMISSIBLE FMLA ABSENCES

In administering any FMLA policy, it must be understood which employee absences are permissible and not permissible. This information is necessary to determine whether the FMLA leave should be approved or denied. Covered FMLA absences may include:

1. The birth, adoption, or foster placement of a child;

2. Prenatal care;

3. The employee's need to care for a family member; i.e., a spouse, parent, or child, with a serious health condition; provided that a medical certification of the family member's condition is obtained;

4. The employee's overnight hospitalization;

5. A condition that renders the employee unable to work for at least three calendar days even if two of the three days are weekend days and that the condition required the employee to see a doctor on at least two occasions;

6. Any duration due to a serious health condition requiring regular treatments, for example, one day absences for chemotherapy or for dialysis;

7. Any duration due to required follow-up treatment prescribed by a health care provider, for example, physical therapy or prescription drug treatment;

8. Any duration due to a chronic condition, including asthma, diabetes, and epilepsy; and

9. Any duration due to a permanent or long-term condition for which treatment may not be effective, for example, Alzheimer's disease, a severe stroke, or the terminal stages of a disease.

The FMLA excludes the following conditions unless they become serious health conditions:

1. Common cold;

2. Flu;

3. Upset stomachs;

4. Headaches other than migraines; and

5. Routine dental problems.

D.   DRAFTING FMLA LEAVE POLICIES

In drafting FMLA leave policies, the following should be considered:

1. Applicable federal, state, and local statutory requirements;

2. Employee eligibility requirements;

3. Medical certification prior to and upon return to work;

4. Substitution of any paid leave;

5. Coordination with other group health plan benefits:

   a. Disability leave;

   b. Sick leave;

   c. Vacation leave; or

   d. Workers' Compensation;

6. Time length of leave;

7. Intermittent or leave on a reduced work schedule;

8. Additional leave beyond FMLA leave:

   a. Eligibility:

      i. Males;

      ii. Females; or

      iii. Spouses (only one or both);

   b. Leave's purpose;

   c. Time length;

   d. Compensation status:

      i. Paid or

      ii. Unpaid;

9. Restoration to the same position or to an equivalent position upon return from leave.

E. FMLA POLICIES

In drafting an FMLA policy, the employer's economic situation and its employment philosophy must be considered; i.e, how broad or narrow of an FMLA policy should it institute. The employer's FMLA policy should be drafted to consider its own unique situation. The policy sample set forth below is only intended as a guideline:

FMLA POLICY

Section 1. *Coverage.* All employees who have been employed by the Company for at least twelve months and have worked at least 1,250 hours within the previous twelve month period are eligible for family and/or medical (FMLA) leave of absence. Employees are eligible to take up to twelve weeks of FMLA leave in any twelve month period under four circumstances. FMLA leave may be taken:

A. Upon the birth of the employee's child;

B. Upon the placement of a child with the employee for adoption or foster care;

C. When the employee must care for a spouse, child, or parent who has a serious health condition; or

D. When the employee cannot perform the functions of his or her position because of a serious health condition.

Section 2. *Leave Eligibility Period.* An employee may take up to twelve weeks of FMLA leave in any twelve month period. The twelve month period is a "rolling" period measured backward from the date an employee uses any FMLA leave.

Section 3. *Definitions.*

A. *Health Care Provider*—A doctor of medicine or osteopathy who is authorized to practice medicine or surgery by the State in which the doctor practices or any other person determined by the Secretary of the United States Department of Labor to be capable of providing health care services.

B. *Equivalent*—Means substantially the same but not exactly equal.

C. *Serious Health Condition*—An illness, injury, impairment, or physical or mental condition that involves:

   1. Inpatient care involving an overnight stay in a hospital, hospice, or residential medical care facility, including any period of incapacity which results in an inability to work, attend school, or perform other regular daily activities due to the serious health condition, or treatment for or recovery from the serious health condition, or any subsequent treatment in connection with this inpatient care; or

   2. Continuing treatment by a health care provider of a serious health condition involving continuing treatment by a health care pro-

vider that includes any one or more of the following:

(a) A period of incapacity involving an inability to work, attend school, or perform other regular daily activities due to the serious health condition; or

(b) Treatment for or recovery from the serious health condition which lasts longer than three consecutive calendar days, and any later treatment or period of incapacity related to the same condition, that also involves:

    i. Two or more treatments by a health care provider, by a nurse or physician's assistant under a health care provider's direct supervision, or by a provider of health care services under orders of or on referral by, a health care provider; or

    ii. Treatment by a health care provider on at least one occasion which results in a regimen of continuing treatment under the supervision of the health care provider.

3. Any period of incapacity because of pregnancy, childbirth, or for prenatal care.

4. Any period of incapacity or treatment for an incapacity due to a chronic serious health condition which:

   (a) Requires periodic visits for treatment by a health care provider, or by a nurse or physician's assistant under direct supervision of a health care provider;

   (b) Continues over an extended time period, including recurring episodes of a single underlying condition; and

   (c) Which may cause episodic periods rather than one continuing period of incapacity, for example, asthma, diabetes, epilepsy, etc.

5. A period of incapacity which is permanent or long-term because of a condition for which treatment may not be effective, for example, Alzheimer's, a severe stroke, or the terminal stages of cancer.

6. Any period of absence to receive multiple treatments, including any period of recovery from those treatments, by a health care provider or by a provider of health care services under orders of, or on referral by, a health care provider, either for restorative surgery after an accident or other injury, or for a condition that would likely cause a period of incapacity of more than three consecutive calendar days if there were no medical intervention or treatment, for example, chemotherapy, radiation, etc. for cancer; physical therapy for severe arthritis; and dialysis for kidney disease.

Section 4. *Coordination with Other Leaves.* All FMLA leaves shall be coordinated with leaves granted under other Company policies. If an employee is entitled to leave under another Company benefit plan or policy, the employee shall take this other leave first, and this leave shall count as part of the twelve weeks of FMLA leave. For example, if an employee has paid vacation leave available, the employee shall take this paid vacation leave, and this leave shall count as part of the twelve weeks of FMLA leave. Likewise, if an employee is entitled to disability leave, the employee shall take the disability leave and this leave shall also count as part or all of the twelve weeks of FMLA leave.

Section 5. *Medical Certification.* The Company will require medical certification to support a claim for FMLA leave for an employee's own serious health condition or to care for a seriously ill spouse, child, or parent. For the employee's own FMLA medical leave, the certification must include a statement that the employee cannot perform the functions of his or her job. For FMLA leave to care for a seriously ill spouse, child, or parent, the certification shall include an estimate of the amount of time the employee will be needed to provide care. In its discretion, the Company may require a second medical opinion and periodic recertification at its expense. If the first and second opinions differ, the Company, at its expense, may require the binding opinion of a third health care provider, approved jointly by the Company and the employee.

Section 6. *Intermittent or Reduced Leave Schedules.* Employees may take FMLA leave on an intermittent or reduced leave schedule, if medically necessary for a serious health condition of the employee or the employee's spouse, child, or parent. If an employee requests FMLA leave on this basis, the Company may require the employee to transfer temporarily to an alternative position which better accommodates recurring periods of absence or a part-time schedule, provided that the position has equivalent pay and benefits.

Section 7. *Both Spouses Employed by the Company.* Spouses who are both employed by the Company may take a total of twelve weeks of FMLA leave in any twelve month period rather than twelve weeks each for the birth, adoption, or foster care placement of a child, or for the care of a sick child or parent.

Section 8. *Group Insurance Continuation During FMLA Leave.*

A. Any employee granted an approved FMLA leave must provide for the retention of his or her group insurance coverages by arranging to pay his or her portion of the premium, if any, during the period of any unpaid absence. For those portions of the FMLA leave which will be paid leave as required under Section 4 "Coordination With Other Leaves", the usual authorized deductions from the employee's pay will be made.

B. If an employee decides not to return to work after completing an FMLA leave, the Company may recover from the employee the cost of any payments the Company made to maintain the employee's insurance coverage, unless the failure to return to work is for reasons beyond the employee's control. For employees who do not return to work after an FMLA leave, the Company will calculate benefit entitlements based upon length of service as of the last paid work day before the leave started.

Section 9. *Employee Request for FMLA Leave/Medical Certification.*

A. *Foreseeable FMLA Leave—Written Notice.* When an employee can foresee the need for FMLA leave, such as leave for birth or adoption of a child or planned medical treatment, the employee shall, if able to do so, give reasonable prior written notice to schedule the leave to not disrupt Company operations. Employees should normally submit FMLA leave requests thirty (30) calendar days before the leave will start.

B. *Reporting While on Leave.* In cases of illness, the employee must report periodically on his or her leave status and intention to return to work.

C. *Requests for FMLA Leaves Involving a Serious Health Condition.* Requests for FMLA leave due to a serious health condition must include the following sufficient medical certification attached to the written leave request:

1. The date when the serious health condition began;

2. The probable duration of the condition; and

3. The appropriate medical facts which the health care provider knows about the condition.

In addition, for leave to care for a spouse, child, or parent, the certification should estimate the time period the employee will need to provide care. For leave for an employee's own serious health condition, the certification must state that the employee cannot perform his or her job functions.

D. *Intermittent Leave or Leave on a Reduced Leave Schedule.* For intermittent leave or leave on a reduced leave schedule for planned medical treatment, the written certification must state the dates when this treatment is planned and how long the treatment will take.

Section 10. *Return to Work After an FMLA Leave.* When an employee returns to active employment from an FMLA leave he or she shall return to the same or an equivalent position with equivalent employee benefits and compensation and other conditions of employment. However, if the employee on FMLA leave is a salaried employee and is among the highest paid ten percent of the employees within 75 miles of the employee's worksite, and keeping the job open for the employee would result in substantial economic injury to the Company, reinstatement to the employee on FMLA leave can be denied. In this situation, the employee will be given an opportunity to return to work before the Company fills the position.

F. FMLA FORMS

The following forms should be considered in administering and notifying employees of their FMLA rights:

1.   EMPLOYEE REQUEST
FOR FMLA LEAVE

Name: _____   Date: _____

Address: _____

_____

Telephone: _____

1. *The type of leave requested.* Please check one:

____ Family and Medical Leave of Absence from
_____ to _____

____ Extension of Family and Medical Leave of Absence   from   _____   to
_____

2. *The Reason for the Family and Medical Leave.* Please check one:

____ My personal serious health condition

____ Birth of my child

_____ Adoption of a child by me

_____ Placement by the state of a child with me for foster care

_____ Serious health condition of my spouse

_____ Serious health condition of my child

_____ Serious health condition of my parent

3. *Full Leave, Intermittent Leave, or Leave on a Reduced Schedule.* Is this leave for (please check one):

_____ Full leave

_____ Intermittent leave

_____ Leave on a reduced work schedule

4. *Medical Certifications.* I agree to provide any medical certification that the Company may request that is permissible under the Family and Medical Leave Act (FMLA) of 1993 to verify, grant, or continue my leave. These medical certifications include the following:

a. Medical Certification—Generally

The Company may require a certification from a health care provider to support and verify FMLA leaves:

  i. To care for the spouse, or a daughter, son, or parent of the employee, if this spouse, daughter, son, or parent has a serious health condition or

  ii. For a serious health condition that makes the employee unable to perform the functions of his or her position.

This certification may be required from a health care provider of the:

    i.   Eligible employee or

    ii.   Spouse, daughter, son, or parent.

The employee must provide a copy of this certification in a timely manner. A certification is generally sufficient if it states:

    i.   The date on which the serious health condition commenced;

    ii.   The condition's probable duration; and

    iii.   The appropriate medical facts within the health care provider's knowledge regarding the condition.

b. Medical Certification—Employee's Care of a Spouse, Daughter, Son, or Parent with a Serious Health Condition

To care for a spouse, daughter, son, or parent of the employee, if this spouse, daughter, son, or parent has a serious health condition, the certification must include:

    i.   The date on which the serious health condition commenced;

    ii.   The condition's probable duration;

    iii.   The appropriate medical facts within the health care provider's knowledge regarding the condition;

    iv.   A statement that the employee is needed to care for the spouse, daughter, son, or parent; and

    v.   An estimate of the amount of time that the employee is needed to care for the spouse, daughter, son, or parent.

c. Medical Certification—Employee's Serious Health Condition

For a serious health condition that makes the employee unable to perform the functions of his or her position, the employee's certification must include:

    i.   The date on which the serious health condition commenced;

    ii.   The condition's probable duration;

    iii.   The appropriate medical facts within the health care provider's knowledge regarding the condition; and

    iv.   A statement that the employee is unable to perform the functions of the position for which he or she is employed.

d. Medical Certification–Intermittent Leave/Reduced Leave Schedule—Employee's Care of a Spouse, Daughter, Son, or Parent with a Serious Health Condition

To care for a spouse, daughter, son, or parent of the employee, if this spouse, daughter, son, or parent has a serious health condition, the certification for intermittent leave or leave on a reduced leave schedule must include a statement indicating:

    i.   That the employee is needed to care for the spouse, daughter, son, or parent who has a serious health condition or will assist in their recovery and

ii. The intermittent leave's or reduced leave schedule's expected duration and schedule.

e. Medical Certification–Intermittent Leave/ Reduced Leave Schedule—Employee's Planned Medical Treatment

Where an employee takes intermittent leave or leave on a reduced leave schedule for planned medical treatment, the employee is required to provide a certification containing:

i. The dates on which the treatment is expected to be given and

ii. The treatment's duration.

f. Medical Certification–Intermittent Leave/ Reduced Leave Schedule—Employee's Serious Health Condition

For a serious health condition that makes the employee unable to perform the functions of his or her position, the employee's certification for intermittent leave or leave on a reduced schedule must include a statement of:

i. The medical necessity for the leave and

ii. The leave's expected duration.

g. Medical Certification—Second Opinion

The Company may require a second opinion from a second health care provider where the employer has reason to doubt the validity of the original certification where the employee's FMLA leave is:

    i.   To care for the spouse, or a daughter, son, or parent of the employee, if this spouse, daughter, son, or parent has a serious health condition; or

    ii.   For a serious health condition that makes the employee unable to perform the functions of his or her position.

In securing the second opinion, the Company is entitled to information relating to:

    i.   The date on which the serious health condition commenced;

    ii.   The condition's probable duration; and

    iii.   The appropriate medical facts within the health care provider's knowledge regarding the condition.

The Company will pay the employee's expense in securing the second opinion. However, the Company may designate the second health care provider or approve the employee's choice of the second health care provider. In neither case, will the health care provider who is engaged to provide the second opinion be employed on a regular basis by the Company.

Where the second opinion differs from the original certification's opinion, the Company may require, at the Company's expense, that the employee obtain a third health care provider's opinion. The third health care provider must be designated or approved jointly by the employee and the Company and must provide information regarding:

i.   The date on which the serious health condition commenced;

ii. The condition's probable duration; and

iii. The appropriate medical facts within the health care provider's knowledge regarding the condition.

Where a third opinion is required, it shall be considered to be final and binding on the employee and the Company.

h. Medical Certification—Subsequent Recertification

The Company may require that the employee obtain subsequent recertifications on a reasonable basis.

5. *Employee Acknowledgment of Leave Request.* I certify that the above information is true and correct to the best of my knowledge. If the Company grants my request for Family and Medical Leave, I agree to comply with the Company's Family and Medical Leave policy. Furthermore, I understand that if I do not comply with the Company's Family and Medical Leave policy I may in the Company's discretion be subject to discipline up to and including termination from employment.

_____

Employee's signature

2.   EMPLOYER'S RESPONSE TO AN EMPLOYEE'S FMLA LEAVE REQUEST

FORM WH–381

PROTOTYPE NOTICE: EMPLOYER RESPONSE TO EMPLOYEE REQUEST FOR FAMILY MEDICAL LEAVE

Employer Response to Employee Request for Family or Medical Leave (*Optional use form—see* 29 CFR § 825.301(c))14

U.S. Department of Labor Employment Standards Administration Wage and Hour Division

(Family and Medical Leave Act of 1993)

(Date)

TO: _____

    (Employee's name)

FROM: _____

     (Name of appropriate employer representative)

SUBJECT: Request for Family/Medical Leave

On _____, you notified us of your need to take

    (date)

family/medical leave due to:

☐ the birth of your child, or the placement of a child with you for adoption or foster care; or

☐ a serious health condition that makes you unable to perform the essential functions of your job; or

☐ a serious health condition affecting your

☐ spouse,

☐ child, or

☐ parent, for which you are needed to provide care

You notified us that you need this leave beginning on _____ (date)

and that you expect leave to continue until on or about _____. (date)

Except as explained below, you have a right under the FMLA for up to 12 weeks of unpaid leave in a 12–month period for the reasons listed above. Also, your health benefits must be maintained during any period of unpaid leave under the same conditions as if you continued to work, and you must be reinstated to the same or an equivalent job with the same pay, benefits, and terms and conditions of employment on your return from leave. If you do not return to work following FMLA leave for a reason other than: (1) the continuation, recurrence, or onset of a serious health condition which would entitle you to FMLA leave; or (2) other circumstances beyond your control, you may be required to reimburse us for our share of health insurance premiums paid on your behalf during your FMLA leave.

This is to inform you that (**check appropriate boxes, explain where indicated**):

1. You are ☐ eligible ☐ not eligible for leave under the FMLA.

2. The requested leave ☐ will ☐ will not be counted against your annual FMLA leave entitlement.

3. You ☐ will ☐ will not be required to furnish medical certification of a serious health condition. If required, you must furnish certification by _____ (*insert date*) (must be at least 15 days after you are notified of this requirement) or we may delay the commencement of your leave until the certification is submitted.

4. You may elect to substitute accrued paid leave for unpaid FMLA leave. We ☐ will ☐ will not require that you substitute accrued paid leave of unpaid FMLA leave. If paid leave will be used the following conditions will apply: (*Explain*)

5. (a). If you normally pay a portion of the premiums for your health insurance, these payments will continue during the period of FMLA leave. Arrangements for payment have been discussed with you and it is agreed that you will make premium payments as follows: (*Set forth dates, e.g., the 10th of each month,*

or pay periods, etc. that specifically cover the agreement with the employee.)

(b). You have a minimum 30–day *(or, indicate longer period, if applicable)* grace period in which to make premium payments. If payment is not made timely, your group health insurance may be cancelled, *provided* we notify you in writing at least 15 days before the date that your health coverage will lapse, or, at our option, we may pay your share of the premiums during FMLA leave, and recover these payments from you upon your return to work. We ☐ will ☐ will not pay your share of health insurance premiums while you are on leave.

(c). We ☐ will ☐ will not do the same with other benefits (e.g. life insurance, disability insurance, etc.) while you are on FMLA leave. If we do pay your premiums for other benefits, when you return from leave you ☐ will ☐ will not be expected to reimburse us for the payments made on your behalf.

6. You ☐ will ☐ will not be required to present a fitness-for-duty certificate prior to being restored to employment. If such certification is required but not received, your return to work may be delayed until the certification is provided.

7. (a). You ☐ are ☐ are not a "key employee" as described in § 825.218 of the FMLA regulations. If you are a "key employee," restoration to employment may be denied following FMLA leave on the grounds that such restoration will cause substantial and grievous economic injury to us.

    (b). We ☐ have ☐ have not determined that restoring you to employment at the conclusion of FMLA leave will cause substantial and grievous economic harm to us. *(Explain (a) and/or (b) below. See § 825.219 of the FMLA regulations.)*

8. While on leave, you ☐ will ☐ will not be required to furnish us with periodic reports every _____ (indicate interval of periodic reports, as appropriate for the particular leave situation) of your status and intent to return to work (see § 825.309 of the FMLA regulations). If the circumstances of your leave change and you are able to return to work earlier than the date indicated on the reverse side of this form, you ☐ will ☐ will not be required to notify us at least two work days prior to the date you intend to report for work.

9. You ☐ will ☐ will not be required to furnish recertification relating to a serious health condition. *(Explain below, if necessary, including the interval between certifications as*

prescribed in § 825.308 of the FMLA regulations.)

3. DEPARTMENT OF LABOR (DOL) FORM FOR CERTIFICATION OF PHYSICIAN OR PRACTITIONER

FORM WH–380

CERTIFICATION OF HEALTH CARE PROVIDER

(FAMILY AND MEDICAL LEAVE ACT OF 1993)

1. Employee's Name:

2. Patient's Name (if different from employee):

3. The attached sheet describes what is meant by a "serious health condition" under the Family and Medical Leave Act. Does the patient's condition[1] qualify under any of the categories described? If so, please check the applicable category.

   (1) ___ (2) ___ (3) ___ (4) ___ (5) ___ (6) ___, or

   None of the above ___

4. Describe the medical facts which support your certification, including a brief statement as to how the medical facts meet the criteria of one of these categories:

---

1. Here and elsewhere on this form, the information sought relates only to the condition for which the employee is taking FMLA leave.

5.   a. State the approximate date the condition commenced, and the probable duration of the condition (and also the probable duration of the patient's present incapacity[2] if different):

    b. Will it be necessary for the employee to take work only **intermittently or to work on a less than full schedule** as a result of the condition (including for treatment described in Item 6 below)? _____

If yes, give the probable duration.

    c. If the condition is a chronic condition (condition #4) or pregnancy, state whether the patient is presently incapacitated[2] and the likely duration and frequency of episodes of incapacity[2]:

6.   a. If additional treatments will be required for the condition, provide an estimate of the probable number of such treatments:

If the patient will be absent from work or other daily activities because of treatment on an **intermittent or part-time** basis, also provide an estimate of the probable number and interval between such treatments, actual or estimated dates of treatment if known, and period required for recovery if any:

    b. If any of these treatments will be provided by another provider of health services (e.g.

---

2. "Incapacity," for purposes of FMLA, is defined to mean inability to work, attend school or perform other regular daily activities due to the serious health condition, treatment therefor, or recovery therefrom.

physical therapist), please state the nature of the treatments:

c. **If a regimen of continuing treatment** by the patient is required under your supervision, provide a general description of such regimen (e.g. prescription drugs, physical therapy requiring special equipment):

7. a. If a medical leave is required for the employee's **absence from work** because of the **employee's own condition** (including absences due to pregnancy or a chronic condition), is the employee unable to perform work of any kind? _____

   b. If able to perform some work, is the employee **unable to perform any one or more of the essential functions of the employee's job** (the employee or the employer should supply you with information about the essential job functions)? _____ If yes, please list the essential functions the employee is unable to perform:

   c. If neither a nor b applies, is it necessary for the employee to be **absent from work for treatment?**

8. a. If leave is required to **care for a family member** of the employee with a serious health condition, **does the patient require assistance** for basic medical or personal needs or safety, or for transportation? _____

b. If no, would the employee's presence to provide **psychological comfort** be beneficial to the patient or assist in the patient's recovery? _____

c. If the patient will need care only **intermittently** or on a part-time basis, please indicate the probable duration of this need:

_____

(Signature of Health Care (Type of Practice)
Provider)

_____

_____   _____

(Address)   (Telephone Number)

To be completed by the employee needing family leave to care for a family member:

State the care you will provide and an estimate of the period during which care will be provided, including a schedule if leave is to be taken intermittently or if it will be necessary for you to work less than a full schedule:

_____   _____

(Employee signature)   (date)

A **"Serious Health Condition"** means an illness, injury, impairment, or physical or mental condition that involves one of the following:

1. Hospital Care

Inpatient care (i.e., an overnight stay) in a hospital, hospice, or residential medical care facility, including any period of incapacity[2] or subsequent treatment in connection with or consequent to such inpatient care.

2. Absence Plus Treatment

a. A period of incapacity[2] of **more than three consecutive calendar days** (including any subsequent treatment or period of incapacity[2] relating to the same condition), that also involves:

(1) **Treatment[3] two or more times** by a health care provider, by a nurse or physician's assistant under direct supervision of a health care provider, or by a provider of health care services (e.g., physical therapist) under orders of, or on referral by, a health care provider; *or*

(2) **Treatment** by a health care provider on at least one occasion which results in a **regimen of continuing treatment[4]** under the supervision of the health care provider.

---

3. Treatment includes examinations to determine if a serious health condition exists and evaluations of the condition. Treatment does not include routine physical examinations, eye examinations, or dental examinations.

4. A regimen of continuing treatment includes, for example, a course of prescription medication (*e.g.*, an antibiotic) or therapy requiring special equipment to resolve or alleviate the health condition. A regimen of treatment does not include the taking of over-the-counter medications such as aspirin, antihistamines, or salves; or bed-rest, drinking fluids, exercise, and other similar

3. Pregnancy

Any period of incapacity due to **pregnancy**, or for **prenatal care**

4. Chronic Conditions Requiring Treatments

A chronic condition which:

(1) Requires **periodic visits** for treatment by a health care provider, or by a nurse or physician's assistant under direct supervision of a health care provider;

(2) Continues over an **extended period of time** (including recurring episodes of a single underlying condition); and

(3) May cause **episodic** rather than a continuing period of incapacity[2] (e.g., asthma, diabetes, epilepsy, etc.).

5. Permanent/Long–Term Conditions Requiring Supervision

A period of **incapacity**[2] which is **permanent or long-term** due to a condition for which treatment may not be effective. The employee or family member must be under the **continuing supervision of, but need not be receiving active treatment by, a health care** provider. Examples include Alzheimer's, a severe stroke, or the terminal stages of a disease.

---

activities that can be initiated without a visit to a health care provider.

6. Multiple Treatments (Non–Chronic Conditions)

Any period of absence to receive **multiple treatments** (including any period of recovery therefrom) by a health care provider or by a provider of health care services under orders of, or on referral by, a health care provider, either for **restorative surgery** after an accident or other injury, or for a condition that would likely **result in a period of incapacity[2] of more than three consecutive calendar days in the absence of medical intervention or treatment**, such as cancer (chemotherapy, radiation, etc.), severe arthritis (physical therapy), kidney disease (dialysis).

4. DEPARTMENT OF LABOR (DOL) FAMILY AND MEDICAL LEAVE ACT (FMLA) FACT SHEET FOR EMPLOYEES

The U.S. Department of Labor's Employment Standards Administration, Wage and Hour Division, administers and enforces the Family and Medical Leave Act (FMLA) for all private, state and local government employees, and some federal employees. Most Federal and certain congressional employees area also covered by the law and are subject to the jurisdiction of the U.S. Office of Personnel Management or the Congress.

FMLA became effective on August 5, 1993, for most employers. If a collective bargaining agreement (CBA) was in effect on that date, FMLA became effective on the expiration date of the CBA or February 5, 1994, whichever was earlier.

FMLA entitles eligible employees to take up to 12 weeks of unpaid, job-protected leave in a 12–month period for specified family and medical reasons. The employer may elect to use the calendar year, a fixed 12–month leave or fiscal year, or a 12–month period prior to or after the commencement of leave as the 12–month period.

The law contains provisions on employer coverage; employee eligibility for the law's benefits; entitlement to leave, maintenance of health benefits during leave, and job restoration after leave; notice and certification of the need for FMLA leave; and, protection for employees who request or take FMLA leave. The law also requires employers to keep certain records.

Employer Coverage

FMLA applies to all:

- public agencies, including state, local and federal employers, local education agencies (schools) and

- private-sector employers who employed 50 or more employees in 20 or more workweeks in the current or preceding calendar year and who are engaged in commerce or in any industry or activity affecting commerce—including joint employers and successors of covered employers.

Employee Eligibility

To be eligible for FMLA benefits, an employee must:

(1) work for a covered employer;

(2) have worked for the employer for a total of 12 months;

(3) have worked at least 1,250 hours over the previous 12 months; and

(4) work at a location in the United States or in any territory or possession of the United States where at least 50 employees are employed by the employer within 75 miles.

Leave Entitlement

A covered employer must grant an eligible employee up to a total of 12 workweeks of unpaid leave during any 12–month period for one or more of the following reasons:

- for the birth and care of the newborn child of the employee;

- for placement with the employee of a son or daughter for adoption or foster care;

- to care for an immediate family member (spouse, child, or parent) with a serious health condition; or

- to take medical leave when the employee is unable to work because of a serious health condition.

Spouses employed by the same employer are jointly entitled to a *combined* total of 12 workweeks of family leave for the birth and care of the newborn child, for placement of a child for adoption or foster care, and to care for a parent who has a serious health condition.

Leave for birth and care, or placement for adoption or foster care must conclude within 12 months of the birth or placement.

Under some circumstances, employees may take FMLA leave intermittently—which means taking leave in blocks of time, or by reducing their normal weekly or daily work schedule.

- If FMLA leave is for birth and care or placement for adoption or foster care, use of intermittent leave is subject to the employer's approval.

- FMLA leave may be taken intermittently whenever *medically necessary* to care for a seriously ill family member, or because the employee is seriously ill and unable to work.

Also, subject to certain conditions, employees or employers may choose to use accrued *paid* leave (such as sick or vacation leave) to cover some or all of the FMLA leave. The employer is responsible for designating if an employee's use of paid leave counts as FMLA leave, based on information from the employee.

"Serious health condition" means an illness, injury, impairment, or physical or mental condition that involves either:

- any period of incapacity or treatment connected with inpatient care (i.e., an overnight stay) in a hospital, hospice, or residential medical-care facility, and any period of incapacity or subsequent treatment in connection with such inpatient care; or

- continuing treatment by a health care provider which includes any period of incapacity (i.e., inability to work, attend school or perform other regular daily activities) due to:

(1) A health condition (including treatment therefor, or recovery therefrom) lasting more than three consecutive days, and any subsequent treatment or period of incapacity relating to the same condition, that also includes:

- treatment two or more times by or under the supervision of a health care provider, or

- one treatment by a health care provider with a continuing regimen of treatment; or

(2) Pregnancy or prenatal care. A visit to the health care provider is not necessary for each absence; or

(3) A chronic serious health condition which continues over an extended period of time, requires periodic visits to a health care provider, and may involve occasional episodes of incapacity (e.g., asthma, diabetes). A visit to a health care provider is not necessary for each absence; or

(4) A permanent or long-term condition for which treatment may not be effective (e.g., Alzheimer's, a severe stroke, terminal cancer). Only supervision by a health care provider is required, rather than active treatment; or

(5) Any absences to receive multiple treatments for restorative surgery or for a condition which would likely result in a period of incapacity of more than three days if not treated (e.g., chemotherapy or radiation treatments for cancer).

"Health care provider" means:

- doctors of medicine or osteopathy authorized to practice medicine or surgery by the state in which the doctors practice; or

- podiatrists, dentists, clinical psychologists, optometrists and chiropractors (limited to manual manipulation of the spine to correct a subluxation as demonstrated by X-ray to exist) authorized to practice, and performing within the scope of their practice, under state law; or

- nurse practitioners and nurse-midwives and clinical social workers authorized to practice, and performing within the scope of their practice, as defined under state law; or

- Christian Science practitioners listed with the First Church of Christ, Scientist in Boston, Massachusetts; or

- Any health care provider recognized by the employer or the employer's group health plan manager.

Maintenance of Health Benefits

A covered employer is required to maintain group health insurance coverage for an employee on FMLA leave whenever such insurance was provided before the leave was taken and on the same terms as if the employee had continued to work. If applicable, arrangements will need to be made for employees to pay their share of health insurance premiums while on leave.

In some instances, the employer may recover premiums it paid to maintain health coverage for an employee who fails to return to work from FMLA leave.

Job Restoration

Upon return from FMLA leave, an employee must be restored to the employee's original job, or to an equivalent job with equivalent pay, benefits, and other terms and conditions of employment.

In addition, an employee's use of FMLA leave cannot result in the loss of any employment benefit that the employee earned or was entitled to before using FMLA leave, nor be counted against the employee under a no fault attendance policy.

Under specified and limited circumstances where restoration to employment will cause substantial and grievous injury to its operations, an employer may refuse to reinstate certain highly-paid "key" employees after using FMLA leave during which health coverage was maintained. In order to do so, the employer must:

- notify the employee of his or her status as a "key" employee in response to the employee's notice of intent to take FMLA leave;

- notify the employee as soon as the employer decides it will deny job restoration and explain the reasons for this decision;

- offer the employee a reasonable opportunity to return to work from FMLA leave after giving this notice;

- and make a final determination as to whether reinstatement will be denied at the end of the leave period if the employee then requests restoration.

A "key" employee is a salaried "eligible" employee who is among the highest paid ten percent of employees within 75 miles of the work site.

Notice and Certification

Employees seeking to use FMLA leave are required to provide 30–day advance notice of the need to take FMLA leave when the need is foreseeable and such notice is practicable.

Employers may also require employees to provide:

- medical certifications supporting the need for leave due to a serious health condition affecting the employee or an immediate family member;

- second or third medical opinions (at the employer's expense) and periodic recertification; and

- periodic reports during FMLA leave regarding the employee's status and intent to return to work.

When intermittent leave is needed to care for an immediate family member or the employee's own illness, and is for planned medical treatment, the employee must try to schedule treatment so as not to unduly disrupt the employer's operation.

Covered employers must post a notice approved by the Secretary of Labor explaining rights and responsibilities under FMLA. An employer that willfully violates this posting requirement may be subject to a fine of up to $100 for each separate offense.

Also, covered employers must inform employees of their rights and responsibilities under FMLA, including giving specific written information on which is required of the employee and what might happen in certain circumstances, such as if the employee fails to return to work after FMLA leave.

Unlawful Acts

It is unlawful for any employer to interfere with, restrain, or deny the exercise of any right provided by FMLA. It is also unlawful for an employer to discharge or discriminate against any individual for opposing any practice, or because of involvement in any proceeding, related to FMLA.

Enforcement

The Wage and Hour Division investigates complaints. If violations cannot be satisfactorily resolved, the Department may bring action in court to compel compliance. Individuals may also bring a private civil action against an employer for violations.

Other Provisions

Special rules apply to employees of local education agencies. Generally, these rules provide for FMLA leave to be taken in blocks of time when intermittent leave is needed or the leave is required near the end of a school term.

Salaried executive, administrative, and professional employees of covered employers who meet the Fair Labor Standards Act (FLSA) criteria for exemption from minimum wage and overtime under Regulations, [29 CFR § 541] 29 CFR Part 541, do not lose their FLSA-exempt status by using any unpaid FMLA leave. This special exception to the "salary basis" requirements for FLSA's exemption extends only to "eligible" employees' use of leave required by FMLA.

The FMLA does not affect any other federal or state law which prohibits discrimination, nor supersede any state or local law which provides greater family or medical leave protection. Nor does it affect an employer's obligation to provide greater leave rights under a collective bargaining agreement or employment benefit plan. The FMLA also encourages employers to provide more generous leave rights.

Further Information

The final rule implementing FMLA is contained in the January 6, 1995, Federal Register. (An interim final rule was published in the Federal Register on June 4, 1993.) For more information, please contact the nearest office of the Wage and Hour Division, listed in most telephone directories under U.S. Government, Department of Labor, Employment Standards Administration.

*

INDEX

References are to Pages

287

BENEFITS—Cont'd
Employee's Payment, 154–157, 178
Employer's Recovery of Benefits Paid, 159–163
Employer's Voluntary Continuation, 158–159
Entitlement to Other Than Group Health Benefits, 153–154
Existing Benefits, 150–152
Insurance Coverage, 214
Maintenance, 157
Multi–Employer Health Plans, 158
New Benefits, 149
Pension and Retirement, 178–179
Preemption of State Regulation, 84–85, 100–102, 222–223
Protection While on Leave, 47, 79–80, 150–152
Requalifying, 177
Types, 175–176
Workers' Compensation Payments, 157

CIVIL RIGHTS ACT OF 1964 (TITLE VII)
See FMLA: An Overview, 54, 87
See Litigation Under the FMLA, 229–230, 240–242

COLLECTIVE BARGAINING AGREEMENTS
See Litigation Under the FMLA, 192

**COMMERCE, INDUSTRY, OR ACTIVITY AFFECTING COM-
MERCE**
Definition, 27–29

COMMISSION ON FAMILY AND MEDICAL LEAVE'S REPORT
Administration Costs, 19–22
Awareness of the FMLA, 16
Duties, 82–84
Employer Communication, 18–19
Employer Leave Policies, 18
Generally, 82–84
Impact on Employee Morale, 17–18
Pre–FMLA Leave Policies, 15–16
Return-to-Work Rate, 19
Use of FMLA Leave, 17

CONGRESSIONAL ACCOUNTABILITY ACT
See FMLA: An Overview, 87

CONGRESSIONAL EMPLOYEES
Complaints, 88–89
Generally, 87–88
Remedies, 89–90

CONSOLIDATED OMNIBUS BUDGET RECONCILIATION ACT OF 1986 (COBRA)
See Benefit and Leave Guidelines Under the FMLA's Regulations, 152, 155, 161, 163

DAMAGES AND REMEDIES
Attorneys' Fees, 194–195
Backpay, 195
Benefits, 195–196
Child Care Costs, 196
Costs, 196
Emotional Distress, 196–197
Employer Liability, 67–68, 89–90
Front Pay, 195
Individual Liability, 213–214
Liquidated Damages, 197
Loss of Job Security, 196
Parental Care Costs, 196
Reduction of the Amount of Liability, 67–68
Punitive Damages, 197–198
Reinstatement; see also Restoration to Position, 198, 173–183, 223–226
Withholding Taxes, 198

DAUGHTER
Definition, 34
Medical Certifications, 40–47, 76–77

DEFINITIONS
Commerce, Industry, or Activity Affecting Commerce, 27–29
Daughter, 34, 70
Eligible Employee, 29, 69
Employ, Employee, State, 29–30
Employer, 30–31
Employment Benefits, 31–32
Health Care Provider, 32, 69
Parent, 33, 70
Person, 33
Reduced Leave Schedule, 33, 69
Secretary, 33
Serious Health Condition, 34, 70
Son, 34, 70
Spouse, 34

DEPARTMENT OF LABOR (DOL)
Enforcement Report, 184–186